no. 22

editors:

•

KEVIN BARRY
TOM DUNNE
EDNA LONGLEY

guest editor: FRANK McGUINNESS

CORK UNIVERSITY PRESS

The Irish Review is a refereed journal. Since it first appeared in 1986 it has established itself as a journal of record. It provides a forum for critical and creative writing in English and Irish. Its editorial policy is pluralist and interdisciplinary; pluralist in its commitment to involving writers from all parts and traditions of the island and from other countries; interdisciplinary in its desire to publish articles on the arts, society, philosophy, history, politics, the environment and science. Our aim is to serve a general rather than a specialist readership.

Published by Cork University Press, 1998

ISSN 0790-7850
ISBN 1 85918 190 2

Cover: Des Keogh and Derbhle Crotty in *Portia Coughlan* by Marina Carr (Abbey Theatre Production, 1996). Photograph by Amelia Stein.

Typeset by Tower Books, Ballincollig, Co. Cork
Printed in Britain by MPG Books Limited, Cornwall

Order Information

Institutional rate, two issues £48.00 / $65.00
Individual rate, two issues £16.00 / $22.00
Single copies £7.95 / $11.00
Subscriptions with payment to:
Cork University Press, Crawford Business Park, Crosses Green, Cork, Ireland.
Payment can be made by cheque, postal order, Access, Visa or Mastercard.
Trade orders are distributed by
Gill & Macmillan Distribution Ltd, Goldenbridge, Inchicore, Dublin, Ireland.
(fax +353 1 454 1688)

The Arts Council
An Chomhairle Ealaíon

The Irish Review receives financial assistance from The Arts Council / An Comhairle Ealaíon and The Arts Council of Northern Ireland

ARTS COUNCIL of Northern Ireland

Contributions are invited from Ireland and abroad — to be sent to

The Editors, *The Irish Review*, Cork University Press, Crawford Business Park, Crosses Green, Cork, Republic of Ireland

Telephone +353 21 902980; Fax +353 21 315329; E-mail corkunip@ucc.ie

Contributors should, in the first instance, provide a typescript. If the article is accepted a disc will be required using Word 6 or a text format (.txt or .rtf), saved as IBM compatible. Please follow style of journal and include a short biographical note.

Contents

For its first five years 1986–90 (Numbers 1–9) *The Irish Review* was published by Cork University Press. From 1991 to 1997 (Numbers 10–21) it was published by the Institute of Irish Studies at Queen's University, Belfast. With this issue (No. 22), in keeping with the editorial policy of maintaining balance and parity between north and south, the journal reverts to being published by Cork University Press. The editors are very grateful to the staff of The Institute of Irish Studies for their work on behalf of the journal.

An Extract from

By the Bog of Cats

(to be performed in the Abbey Theatre, 1998)

MARINA CARR

Act One, Scene One

Lights Up. Dawn. Angel Swane enters with the corpse of a black swan, she trails it after her across the snow. She stops, sings softly.

ANGEL: By the Bog of Cats I finally learned false from true.
Learned too late that it was you and always you.
Left me sore a heart brimful of rue.
By the bogful of cats in the darkling of dew.

GF: [*Who has entered as she sings, stands in the shadows listening.*] Where'd ya get thah song from?

ANGEL: [*Turns to look at him*] Had it since I was a ghirl. Falls from me lips at th'oddest times. Who a'you? haven't seen you around here afore?

GF: I'm a ghost fancier.

ANGEL: A ghost fancier, never heard tell of the like.

GF: Ya never imagine ghosts?

ANGEL: Oh aye, seen them and all.

GF: Round here?

ANGEL: Aye, all long the Bog a Cats.

GF: Well where there be ghosts, there be ghost fanciers.

ANGEL: Thah so. So what do ya do Mr Ghost Fancier? eye up ghosts? Have love affairs with them?

GF: Aye.

ANGEL: You're a strange wan.

GF: Not so strange, see if ya can imagine somethin', it prob'ly exists or will exist or at the very worst shoulda existed.

ANGEL: Thah so.

GF: I've trailed ya a while, whah're ya doin' draggin' the corpse of a swan ahind ya like it was your shada?

ANGEL: Me and this swan has known wan another the longest time. We used play together when I was a child. Wance I was taken away from the Bog a Cats and when I returned years laher, this swan here come swoopin' over the bog to welcome me home, came righ' up to me and kissed me hand. And I thought everywan would've forgotton me and everywan had ceptin her, she comes right up to me and we go inta an eye lock, ever locked eyes with a swan Mr Ghost Fancier? Was like she was sayin, though everywan else may have forgotton ya, I have amimbered ya and will for always. And now she's dead, found her frozed on the ice of a boghole, had ta rip her from the ice, left half her underbelly.

GF: No wan ever tell ya it's dangerous t'interfere with swans, most especially black wans?

ANGEL: Only an auld superstition to keep people afraid. Me and this swan understood wan another, like sisters we were, I only want to bury her, she woulda buried me if ih was the other way around.

GF: Yah live in thah caravan?

ANGEL: Used to. Live up the road now. I've me own house, though I can't say I've ever really cared for livin' in it, buh I've a daugher, Josie, she's seven and I've a man I've loved this fourteen year, a dreamer sourt of a man, indecisive as the wind. He built the house for me, buh we're noh gettin' on too well righ' now, buh we'll be fine, jus a phase. Jus a phase. Thah's why I go walkin' ah nigh, to try and figure it all ouh. Buh you Mr Ghost Fancier, whah ghost are ya ghoulin' for round here?

GF: If she'll come with me, her name is Angel Swane.

ANGEL: I'm Angel Swane.

GF: You're Angel Swane! But you're alive.

ANGEL: I certaintly am and aim to stay thah way.

GF: A'ya sure?

ANGEL: What ya mane am I sure, a cuurse I'm sure, I have everythin' to live for.

GF: Thah may be so Angel Swane buh you can asplaine to me how word has reached the other world thah you had landed. I've never been wrong afore.

ANGEL: Well this time y'are ya big swadge of a devil bully ya. Ya come ghostin' across the Bog a Cats into the world of mortals where you've no business. I know your kind. I've wrestled with yees afore. Lave me be!

GF: Is this sunrise or sunseh?

ANGEL: It's wah the old weather diviners do call crepuscular hour, when it could be aither dawn or dusk, the light bein' so similar. Buh it's dawn, there's the sun comin' up.

GF: So it's dawn. Then I'm too previous, I mistook this hour for dusk. A thousand apologies.

ANGEL: Too previous for whah?

GF: I'm sorry.

[*exit GF*]

ANGEL: Too previous for whah.

[*Quietly to herself*]

Scene Four

Enter Angel by the caravan, she digs a grave for the swan. She lays it in the grave and begins shovelling clay in. Enter the Catwoman, a woman in her fifties, old coat, wellingtons, bits of things hanging, dishevelled, catlike.

CATWOMAN: [*Singing. We hear her before we see her.*] Me mother were a tiger, me father a cheehah from the pakes a the Himalayas, me brother were a . . .

[*Stops, looks at Angel Swane.*]

ANGEL: What ya want cahwoman?

CATWOMAN: Whah're ya doin' there?

ANGEL: None a your concern.

CATWOMAN: Buryin' the black swan, sure didn't I see the pair a yees slow dancin all nigh', over by the lee pond, mistook ya for some lonely ghost ah first.

ANGEL: Ya natin' behher ta do than spyin' on me.

CATWOMAN: Wasn't spyin' on ya, jus makin' sure all is as ih should be on the Bog a Cats. I'm the kaper a the Bog a Cats in case ya forgotton. I own this bog.

ANGEL: Ya own natin' Cahwoman cept your little house a turf and your hundred odd mousetraps and anythin' ya can rob. And I'm missin' a garden chair, so ya behher bring ih back or I'll go down meself and blow your little turf house down.

CATWOMAN: Ya wouldn't dare.

ANGEL: I'll bring down fireligher, burn ya ouh.

CATWOMAN: No call for thah sourt a rudeness, I'll bring back your auld garden chair though ya won't be needin' ih no more.

ANGEL: Wonten I now?

CATWOMAN: I had a drame abouh you las nigh'.

ANGEL: Don't wanta hear ih.

CATWOMAN: Dreamt ya were a black train mohorin' through the Bog a Cats and oh the scorch offa this train and ih blastin' by and all the bog be dark.

Y'even quinched the jack a lantern, me partichular friend and I had ta run from the burn. Angel Swane you'll bring this place down afore evensong.

ANGEL: No wan ever tell ya Cahwoman, your drames is abouh yourself, so stop tryin' ta pawn thim off on me.

CATWOMAN: A saucer a milk and none a your cheek?

ANGEL: I've no milk here, ya may go up ta the house ta geh your saucer a milk. Can't see why ya can't drink from a cup like the rest a the world.

CATWOMAN: I toult ya a thousand times ih's acause in Agypt I'm a Quane.

ANGEL: Then why'd'n ya go an back ta Agypt?

CATWOMAN: I will. I will. I sih on a throne there with kohl in me eyes and ever Tom cah in the place squallin' for me.

[*Takes a mouse out of her pocket, raises it up by the tail, eyeballs it, ambiguous as to whether she is going to take a bite out of it.*]

ANGEL: Toult ya I don't want ya handlin' mice around me, dirty auld yokes, full a disases.

CATWOMAN: And you aren't, you clane as snow or whah Angel Swane?

ANGEL: Clane as the next.

CATWOMAN: I knew your mother Angel Swane, I helped her bring ya inta the world, I knew ya whin ya were dribblin' in the coh, seen ya chained like a rabied pup ta this auld caravan. So if I handle a mouse or two, ih's none a your business, righ!

ANGEL: Righ.

CATWOMAN: Now ya've me all upseh so I forgoh whah I came here ta tell ya.

ANGEL: Then tell me abouh me mother for whah I amimber don't seem righ'.

CATWOMAN: What ya amimber and I'll tell ya if'n ya amimber wrong.

ANGEL: Bangles be whah I amimber most, the jangles of her bangles. Usen't she wear wan on her fooh?

CATWOMAN: Aye with bells hangin' offa thim.

ANGEL: And most of all whah I amimber be her pausin'.

CATWOMAN: She was a great wan for the pausin'.

ANGEL: You g'wan ta bed now, she'd say, I'm just pausin'. And I'd watch her from the winda. Times she'd smoke a cigar which she had her own partichular way a doin'. She'd hould it stretched away from her and insteada takin' the cigar to her mouh, she'd take her mouh ta the cigar. I think mebbe for her thim quieh hours pausin on the Bog a Cats was the heigh' a pleasure the world have allohed her. Whah was she waitin' for Catwoman? Whah was she waitin' for?

CATWOMAN: Be the Bog a Cats I dreamed a dream a wooin'
I heard your clear vice ta me a callin'

Thah I must go though ih be my undoin'
Be the Bog a Cats I'll stay no more a ruein'.

[*Sings it*]

Wan a the songs your mother made.

ANGEL: I know it.

CATWOMAN: Ya'd often hear her vice comin' over the bog ah nigh. She was a songstitcher, the greahest of all the songstitchers this place have known and we've had songstitchers a plinty here, buh she was a songstitcher who somewhere along the way lost the weave of the song and in so doin' became small and bihher and mane. I grew ta noh like her ah all.

ANGEL: There's a longin' in me for her thah wont quell this while gone.

CATWOMAN: I'll tell ya a story abouh Josie Swane, the songstitcher, ih concerns you. On the nigh ya were born she taken ya over ta the black swan's lair and lain ya there in her nest aside her. I axed her why. Acause Swane manes swan says your mother and in Irish it's nic ealaion, daugher of a swan. Thah may be so says I, buh the child'll die of pneumonia. Thah child, says Josie Swane will live as long as the black swan, noh a day more, noh a day less. And every nigh' for three nigh's she taken ya ta the black swan's lair and left ya there till dawn.

ANGEL: Ya've no righ' tellin me a story like thah. You're makin' ih up ta geh rid a me like everywan else. Xavier Cassidy put ya up ta this!

CATWOMAN: I'm noh makin' ih up Angel, wishin' if I was. And here's whah I came ta tell ya, lave this place now or ya never will.

ANGEL: Don't seem ta make much differ whether I lave or stay with a curse like thah on me head.

CATWOMAN: There's ways round curses. If ya lave now you'll be allrigh' had a vision abouh ih.

ANGEL: Visions! Visions! I've had me share a visions too!

CATWOMAN: Then heed thim.

ANGEL: I can't! They're too terrible. They're all butchery and carnage. There's somethin' evil has moved in on me blood Cahwoman and it have me afraid, ih's flappin' there in the basement a me heart like a trapped crow or a cornered badger. I can feel its teeth, glistenin away down there in thah dark stinkin' cave, jaws open, ready ta pounce and rip chunks ouha me soul and whin thah happens I wont know who I am anymore.

CATWOMAN: If'n ya lave now you'll be arrigh'.

ANGEL: I'm noh lavin'! Give up everythin' I've battled for?

CATWOMAN: And I'm tellin' ya ya have ta. Whin've I ever been proved wrong? Hah? Toult ya ya'd have just the wan daugher, toult ya the day and the hour she'd be born. Didn't I now?

ANGEL: Aye, ya did.

CATWOMAN: Toult ya Carthage Kilbride were no good for ya, never grew hees back bone, would ya listen? Toult Monica Curly ta stop her only son drivin' ta cihy thah nigh'. Would she listen? Where be her son? In hees grave, thah's where he be, begged her till she ran me off wih a kittle a bilin' waher. Mayhap she wanted him dead. I'll say natin'. In Agypt she be hung or buried alive for defyin' the Cahwoman, Quane a cats. Gev auld Xavier Cassidy herbs ta cure hees wife. Whah'd he do? Pegged thim down the tileh and taken Olive Cassidy ta see some swanky medicine man in a privahe hospital. They cured her allrigh', cured her so well she came back dead as a side a ham in a oak choffin with golden handles. Mebbe he wanted her dead too for ta have more eyeroom ta ogle hees daugher. Bees many as wants their loved wans dead. Thah a fact Angel Swane. People. In Agypt we think different. I'll be off now and don't say the Cahwoman never toult ya. Lave this place now or ya never will.

ANGEL: You've been as often wrong as you've been righ' Cahwoman. I'm stoppin' here.

CATWOMAN: Sure I know thah too, seen it wrih in a boghole.

ANGEL: Be there anythin' ya don't see wrih in a boghole?

CATWOMAN: Sneer away Angel Swane and we'll see be thah sneer on your puss tanigh'. Amimber the Cahwoman then for I don't think I'll have the stomach for this place tanigh'.

[*And exit the Catwoman singing.*]

Me mother were a cheehah from Borneo, me father a Tom chah from Cairo Town.

[*And exit Angel.*]

Scene Seven

Enter Josie Kilbride on a walking stick and with an old shawl around her face. She is playacting at being her granny.

JOSIE: Good mornin' Tinker Swane.

ANGEL: [*Mock surprise*] Oh, Good mornin' Mrs Kilbride? Whah a lovely surprise, and how are ya taday?

JOSIE: I've been savin' all nigh'.

ANGEL: Have ya Mrs Kilbride?

JOSIE: Tell me ya jezebel witch how much have you in the bank taday?

ANGEL: Oh I've three greah big goose eggs Mrs Kilbride. How much have you in the bank?

JOSIE: Seventeen million pound. Seventeen million pound. I saved ih. I didn't frig ih away on love stories and silk stockins. I cuh back on sugar and I cuh back on flour. I drank biled biled socks instead of tae, and in wan nigh' I saved seventeen million pound.

ANGEL: Ya drank biled socks Mrs Kilbride?

JOSIE: I did and I had turf stew for me dinner and for me desert I had snail tart and a big mug of wee wee.

ANGEL: Sounds delicious Mrs Kilbride.

JOSIE: Ya wouldn't geh behher in Buckin'ham Palace.

ANGEL: Josie don't ever say any a thah in front a your Granny sure ya wont?

JOSIE: A cuurse I wont.

ANGEL: Did ya have your breakfast?

JOSIE: I had a sugar sammige.

ANGEL: Ya didn't?

JOSIE: I had cornflakes.

ANGEL: Good ghirl. Did ya wash your teeth?

JOSIE: Forgoh.

ANGEL: Ya'll never be leh inta God's sweetshop if your teeth is rotton. G'wan in and wash thim now.

JOSIE: Tell me abouh God's sweetshop?

ANGEL: Ah Josie, toult ya loads a times.

JOSIE: Ah Mam, jus wance more.

ANGEL: Arrigh', C'mere.

[*Sits her up on her knee.*]

In God's sweetshop there be thousands and thousands a rooms...

JOSIE: No, start at the beginin' abouh how you geh to ih.

ANGEL: The road ta God's sweetshop is thah the part ya mane?

JOSIE: Aye.

[*Listens with open-mouthed wonder.*]

ANGEL: The road ta God's sweetshop is med from toffee so ya have ta wear special shoes ta walk on thah road. . . .

JOSIE: And the shoes is med ouha ice crame.

ANGEL: Thah's righ. So ya walk along the road a toffee in your ice crame shoes and if'n ya want ya can take a lick of your shoe or a suck of the road. And then ya come to a duur med of pink chocolah. . . .

JOSIE: The front duur of God's sweetshop.

ANGEL: Aye and ya knock on the duur?

JOSIE: Could ya take a bite ouha the duur?

ANGEL: Sure ya could if'n ya wanted and ya knock on the duur . . .

JOSIE: And Pollonio the boss of God's sweetshop opens the duur, and she's tiny, only thah size.

[*Indicates size.*]

ANGEL: And ya take Pollonio up in the palm of your hand.

JOSIE: Ya could squash her.

[Squashes the imaginary Pollonio.]

ANGEL: Ya could if ya weren't careful. And what's the first thing Pollonio says?

JOSIE: Show me your teeth?

ANGEL: And you've ta show her your teeth.

[Angel and Josie bare their teeth.]

And she's there in the palm of your hand lookin' righ inta your mouh. And then ya've ta open your mouh wide. . . .

JOSIE: *[Mouth wide open.]* Like this?

ANGEL: Wider. Thah's ih. And Pollonio goes inta your mouh and walks all over your teeth checkin' thim and then she stands on your tongue and looks up at your top teeth. . . .

JOSIE: And ya've ta be careful ya don't swally her or drown her with spittle.

ANGEL: Ya do and then she says, Josie Kilbride you've the most beauhiful teeth in paradise, ya can have all the sweets ya want and you say?

JOSIE: I'll have a bag a gobstoppers, twinty black jacks, four curly wurlies, a loop the loop, a large bottle a coke and a trailer load of penny bars.

ANGEL: And then ya sih in the playground at the back of God's sweetshop and ya chew ta your little hearts contint.

JOSIE: Tell me the bih abouh the chocolah thah's med ouha moon beams.

ANGEL: Laher. Laher. I'm tired Josie.

Drama Publishing

PEGGY BUTCHER

In 1997, the playscript of Brian Friel's *Philadelphia, Here I Come* sold a total of 25,000 copies across Ireland and Britain. Yes, that's right: 25,000 copies of a playscript. It's a common misconception that plays don't sell, that play publishing is a slightly odd and altruistic branch of the profession. After all, surely the play lives in production, on stage, and a mere reading of the text can hardly give more than a faint idea of the exciting meld of text, performers and audience which makes good theatre. But what if you've missed the play in performance? What if you're studying it at school or college? What if you're running a youth theatre group and are searching for new, exciting work to put on locally? Or even, what if you have seen the play and enjoyed it so much you'd like to read it – or perhaps it's teased your imagination and you'd like another look at it, this time on the page?

But yet, 25,000 copies sounds like a bestseller, so how come we don't see Friel, Stoppard, Pinter and Beckett on the much hyped bestseller lists? After all, lifetime sales of the most successful of these writers' plays would make even Martin Amis feel jealous. But the difference with plays is that although they don't sell vast numbers in the space of a week, they do sell well over a period of time. In publishing parlance, fiction is 'frontlist' – which means that it should sell in large quantities over a short period. However, if a novel doesn't sell in the first few months of publication, then the returns from bookshops to the publisher's warehouse will be fast and numerous. A play, however, is 'backlist' – it moves more slowly and in fewer numbers and the plays that go into shops usually stay there for some time. Part of the reason for this is that the novel will be reviewed and hyped and people will buy at that moment. But the play lives in production and it's the play on stage that makes the media splash – rarely the playscript. Yet they do sell. So who buys them?

Generally speaking, new plays sell most during the production of that play. If they happen to be on at the National Theatre in London, then it's possible to sell 50 to a 100 a night at their bookshop, although for more sales than that you'd probably need to be called Stoppard. Other theatres, even those without bookshops, now sell plays in quantities. David Hare's *Amy's View*, for example, sold 135 copies at the theatre alone in its first week in January 1998 at the Aldwych in London. For the traditional book trade, though, a new play usually slides gently into bookshops: a couple in a Dillons here, half a dozen to a Waterstones there, and so on. A new play by an established writer usually means a hike in sales of their earlier plays. In keeping with the idea of 'backlist' publishing, plays stay on the shelves of bookshops and in publishers' warehouses for months or even years, so a new and successful play can sell the playwright's previous work too.

But none of this explains the 25,000 of the Friel in one year. The answer: set texts in schools. Once a play makes it onto the syllabus as a set text, the examination board writes to the publisher to ensure that the play will remain in print for the allotted period. The publisher is delighted to oblige; set texts mean guaranteed sales. In Ireland, a major wholesaler or an educational company will take up 10,000 copies if a play is on a syllabus.

With a well established drama list, Faber and Faber has a high percentage of plays on the set text list as well as a number of writers on the 'recommended reading' list in Ireland and Britain: Beckett, Alan Bennett, Steven Berkoff, Sean O'Casey, Anne Devlin, T.S. Eliot, Brian Friel, Trevor Griffiths, David Hare, Frank McGuinness, John Osborne, Harold Pinter, Tom Stoppard and Timborlake Wertenbaker – all enjoy sales of one or more of their plays into the secondary education market. And it doesn't stop there, these playwrights are joined by others like Sam Shepard, Sharman MacDonald, Christopher Hampton, Simon Gray, Athol Fugard and Philip Ridley, all of whose work is studied in colleges and universities. When it comes to this tertiary level, then collections rather than single plays come in useful. Add in sales to the college markets in America, Canada, Australia, and other English speaking or English as a second language countries, and the sales figures begin to be understandable. From the publishers' viewpoint this also allows some useful marketing to come into play. With thirty titles on the list and more to come, the cohesive and chic look of the collections such as the Faber Contemporary Classics series includes the very different work of many major playwrights. This means that those collections will certainly sell individually but can also be effectively displayed as a group.

So, with lifetime sales running into hundreds of thousands for the best known plays of Beckett, Stoppard, Friel and Pinter, things look very good for the long established playwrights and their publishers. But what of the younger and less well known writers? How do their plays get published? First-time playwrights can be published in one of two ways: the anthology or the single play. A very successful anthology, *The Dazzling Dark: New Irish Plays*, selected and introduced by Frank McGuinness, was published in 1995 and contains work by Marina Carr, Gina Moxley, Jimmy Murphy and Tom MacIntyre. Why were these writers chosen and why is the volume successful in terms of sales? First, the plays are *all* very good. This may seem so obvious as to be hardly worth mentioning, but a glance along bookshelves at short story anthologies usually reveals a few top-class pieces carrying a greater number of less successful works.

Another useful possibility is to have an anthology linked to a prestigious theatre. This has worked very well in the case of the Royal Court in London where their wide-ranging Youth Theatre project in 1994 formed the basis of the *Coming on Strong* volume with four plays by up-and-coming young writers including Kevin Coyle from Derry, Rebecca Prichard from Essex, Nick Crosso from London, and the Liverpudlian Michael Wynne. A youth theatre project with different aspirations makes up the bumper collection published with the National Theatre in 1997. *New Connections: New Plays for Young People* contains twelve plays by writers with a track record of writing, although not always for the stage. Every two years, the National Theatre funded by British Telecom commissions a dozen writers to write plays for young people and, across Britain and Ireland, 150 youth and school theatre groups participate. It's an extraordinary and ambitious scheme which sees dozens of performances of the plays across the two countries in schools, village halls and local theatres. The most interesting groups – one for each play – then bring their production to the National Theatre where each play is seen once in a glorious, celebratory week. Some of the highlights of the week have been Gina Moxley's hilarious and heart-rending *Dog House* performed by Lagan College, Belfast, Philip Ridley's splendid *Sparkleshark*, presented by Belfast's Youth Lyric group, and the poet Simon Armitage's beautifully elliptical *Eclipse* performed by Droichead Youth Theatre. To sit in the National Theatre, packed with hundreds of young people enjoying these shows was a true celebration of theatre. The resulting book contains not only all twelve plays but interviews with the authors and production notes for teachers and youth groups.

Whether an anthology or a single playtext, it is essential that the plays have had, or be about to have, a stage production before being considered for publication. With one or two exceptions, playwrights, particularly those with less experience, go through extensive rewrites during the rehearsal period. This isn't because they don't know their craft but simply once the play is off the page and 'on its feet' on stage, the shortcomings of certain scenes – too long, too short, in the wrong place, no development, no content, impractical in terms of costume changes – become obvious and changes must be made. A publisher does a playwright no favours by putting work into print before the possibility of a production irons out and perfects the play as seen on stage. Fortunately, current technology allows a play to be transferred from the writer's disk to the printed page in less than two weeks if necessary. This will allow those vital rehearsal changes to be made before publication.

But what if a play is about to be produced at a less well known venue and there doesn't happen to be an anthology it would easily slot into? How, then, does a new writer get a play in a single volume without the benefit of a well known name or a prestigious theatre? The answer here goes back to playtext sales in theatres and, in this case, the advent of the programme/playscript. Some thirty years ago, at the Royal Court Theatre, London, the programme/playscript was born. The idea is simple and very effective: both programme and play are bound together in one book. The programme contains all the usual elements, cast list, biographies, notes on the play, advertisements. Rather than being a separate, glossy – or not so glossy – adjunct to the work being performed, the programme takes the first dozen or so pages and the programme/playscript is sold at the theatre at a fraction of what would be the play's retail cost. People go to the theatre, see the play and buy the programme/playscript. It works because the theatre (or touring theatre company) agrees to take a set number of books. The minimum initial sale to the theatre is 500 but it can be as many as 5,000, depending on how many the theatre thinks it can sell. The selling price to the theatre is agreed between publisher and theatre. The deal is done on a firm sale basis, that's to say that the theatre cannot return any unsold books at the end of the play's run. The advantages: the playgoer gets a programme as well as the play for a fraction of the retail price; the theatre gets its usual advertising revenue in the programme as well as making a profit on its initial outlay by charging slightly more to sell the programme/playscript than it paid to buy it; the publisher sells a great many more copies than usual of a relatively unknown playwright's work (albeit at a much lower price) and the work is bought and read by many more people than if it were only sold in bookshops. This is all well and good, but not everyone will be able to get to see a play in Dublin or London or New York, so the programme/playscript will also be sold in bookshops in the usual way for those people who missed the stage production but want to read it for pleasure, study or as a possibility for a second production.

So far we've considered original plays by established and new writers, but what of the large body of plays in translation? Different publishers have different criteria for translations. At Faber and Faber, translations are usually only published where the translator is already an established playwright on the list. It's a good argument that if you want a lucid and actable translation, you must go to someone who knows his or her craft well. This means that the Faber list boasts translations or versions of Ibsen, Chekhov, Sophocles, Racine, and Ionesco by Frank McGuinness, Tom Stoppard, Ted Hughes, David Hare, Martin Crimp, Timberlake Wertenbaker and Trevor Griffiths. A rare treat then to get two writers for the price of one! However, with an eye to the lucrative syllabus market, other publishers will go for a more academic approach. The simple key here is to look out for the words 'translated by' or 'version by'. Translations versus versions opens up a debate – sometimes furious – about the ability of the academic translator to render a play speakable and playable rather than simply readable for study, and the ability of the professional writer, who doesn't speak the original language, truly to render the play as written. Not all writers speak the language of the original work fluently but whereas the academic translator may argue for a close and accurate translation direct from the original, the 'version' writer, whether playwright or poet, will argue the necessity of writing to the spirit of the play but bringing in his or her own understanding of that spirit. Of course, some playwrights, like Michael Frayn, do speak the original language but each translator will find his or her own way into the work. It may not be possible to resolve the basic argument. However, if you've ever thought that the play is the play, no matter who translates it, take a look at a number of translations and versions and notice how they differ.

If you have a drama list full of established and new playwrights, it makes sense to develop a theatrebooks list which will complement that work and present a framework within which to view the plays. There are any number of possibilities here but, to begin with, there's a clear line from the plays to a reading of those plays, either by the playwright or by someone else. Beckett's *Notebooks* are fascinating and give the reader an understanding of the process of writing and revising from one of this century's great writers. An extension of this idea, but with a different focus, comes from biography and autobiography which will often give an enjoyable anecdotal slant on a writer's work. Michael Billington's admired volume, *The Life and Work of Harold Pinter,* provides an overview of all of Pinter's work, enhanced by interviews with the writer, his friends and colleagues. Any fan of Pinter's work would also want to own *Various Voices*, Pinter's selection of his prose, poetry and political writings. Steven Berkoff's entertaining *Free Association* is an autobiographical account of the life of the writer/actor/director and goes some way towards an understanding of the wayward genius which is Berkoff. Readers interested in Alan Bennett's work can find a critical appreciation in *Alan Bennett: In a Manner of Speaking*. These books will soon be joined by Humphrey Carpenter's work on Dennis Potter. All these books form a solid and comprehensive backdrop to the published playlist.

Treading a fine line between general interest and academic usefulness, Open University lecturer Lizbeth Goodman has put together a wide-ranging international collection of plays and performance pieces by women, and includes work by Caryl Churchill, Jackie Kay, Sarah Daniels, Timberlake Wertenbaker and Jamaica Kincaid. *Mythic Women/Real Women* provides a wealth of performance pieces as well as being a provocative primer for women's studies and theatre studies.

But a good theatrebooks list should also consider other aspects of making theatre. A series of 'how-to' books draws on the experiences of professionals and allows a way in for amateurs and would-be practitioners. *On Directing* is a series of interviews with very different directors, including Jonathan Miller, Deborah Warner, Simon McBurney, Katie Mitchell and David Glass. A more in-depth view of a director's work is gained from *A Director Calls* which looks at the Royal Court's Stephen Daldry and his work in theatre.

From directors to actors, useful tips on acting are contained in David Mamet's anarchic text, *True and False*, which tells the aspiring performer what they don't teach you at acting school. Effective use of the voice is essential for an impressive performance on stage or addressing an audience in the lecture room and help is provided by voice teacher Michael McCallion's *The Voice Book*. In simple and practical terms this book shows you how to use your voice freely, powerfully and with pleasure. With school and youth theatre groups abounding, *Dramatic Events: Workshops* provides an exploration of drama techniques within an educational setting, in personal development and in the making of theatre. Anyone who has ever read Keith Johnstone's classic text on improvisation, *Impro*, will be delighted to hear that *Impro for Storytellers* will be joining an updated *Impro* on the Faber list during 1998.

Connecting theatre and children and selling into that market is usually done by specialist educational publishers and Samuel French. However, if you have playwrights on the list who write for children as well as adults (Alan Ayckbourn, for example) then it is useful to make a feature of this part of the drama list. In this way, a choice selection of titles can then be complemented by a book for teachers. Some of the books on the Faber list include the *New Connections* volume, the dramatisations of the Grimm Brothers stories in *Grimm Tales and More Grimm Tales*, Alan Ayckbourn's and Philip Ridley's collections, or Ted Hughes's selection of *Sacred Earth Dramas*. If you want to produce these plays or perhaps write your own, the essential and complete guide to writing, adapting, acting and directing is found in *Theatre for Children* by the master practitioner of children's theatre, David Wood.

And to end where many people begin: with Shakespeare. There are many educational publishers offering Shakespeare's plays, with detailed notes for study. However, if you're going to see a Shakespeare play and need a quick reminder of the main characters and plot, then *A Pocket Guide to Shakespeare's Plays* provides all this and more in a concise, readable one-volume guide to all thirty-eight plays.

Every publisher of drama will have a different selection of playwrights and theatrebooks. An educational publisher will have a clear line to schools and colleges with titles which will sell to those specialist markets. A commercial publisher, such as Faber and Faber, will be delighted to sell into the educational field where possible but must always be mindful of the potential general reader, the occasional and the dedicated playgoer, the amateur, the aspiring and the professional theatre practitioner. As well as publishing plays, a rounded drama list will focus on building a cohesive theatrebooks list which draws on the work of the playwrights on that list as well as broadening out to include other aspects of making theatre. From the selection of titles mentioned earlier, I hope to have given a flavour of a successful and growing list of new playwrights joining the established and prestigious playwrights already published as well as giving an indication of how a living theatrebooks list might grow.

For those who have their own ideas for a useful book on drama and are wondering how to go about approaching a publisher the first thing to do is to go to a good bookshop and see what's available in the particular area you're considering. If there are already several other books, what will make yours different? Check who publishes what. What seems to be the focus of that list? If a publisher already has a book on that aspect of theatre, they probably won't want another. However, if a publisher seems to have a gap in that area, perhaps your idea will fit in well. A quick phonecall will ascertain whether or not your idea is viable, although tread carefully, some publishers prefer everything in writing. When you do come to putting your proposal in writing, make sure you've done your homework first. It's no good sending your university thesis to a commercial publisher but it might be of interest to an educational publisher. Get the current catalogues from all the interesting publishers. From these you can see not only who they publish but what their markets are and how they perceive and advertise themselves. Couch your proposal in terms that will appeal to that publisher. It's useful to think of a book proposal as rather like a job application. If you're applying for several jobs there will be certain common aspects of your application but if you're doing it singly you'll tailor each one specifically. One general book proposal sent to several publishers is not good enough. Consider it from the point of view of each drama editor and rework it to suit.

An Extract from
The Wild Duck

(to be performed in the Abbey Theatre, 1999)

Translated by
FRANK McGUINNESS

Act Three

Morning in Hjalmar Ekdal's studio. Daylight comes through the large sky-light. The curtain has been pulled back. Hjalmar sits by his table retouching a photograph. Several other photographs lie in front of him. Wearing a hat and coat Gina enters through the front door. On her arm she has a lidded basket.

HJALMAR: Gina, you're back already?

GINA: Yes, I hurried myself along.

[*She puts down the basket and takes off the hat and coat.*]

HJALMAR: Did you look in on Gregers?

GINA: I did that, yes. It looks really beautiful in there. He's really made that room look lovely.

HJALMAR: Has he?

GINA: Yes, he wanted to do it all himself. He put logs in the stove and then closed the clamper, so the whole room was choked with smoke. The smell –

HJALMAR: He didn't?

GINA: Wait for it – he wanted to put the fire out, so he throws water into the stove and of course the floor was covered in filth, absolutely covered.

HJALMAR: That's annoying.

GINA: I had to get the porter's wife to scrub up after him, the pig. It's not fit to go into until the afternoon.

HJALMAR: So what's he doing with himself in the meantime?

GINA: He said he'd go out for a while.

HJALMAR: I popped in to see him – after you left.

GINA: I heard. You've asked him in to lunch.

HJALMAR: Just a bite to eat, you know. It's his first day – we have to. You've always got something nice in the house.

GINA: I'll have to find something.

HJALMAR: Don't be too sparing. I think Relling and Holvik will be coming as well. I've just bumped into Relling on the stairs, so I had to –

GINA: Those two as well?

HJALMAR: Good God, two more – what difference does it make?

[*Old Ekdal opens the door – looks in.*]

EKDAL: Hjalmar, are you there?

[*He sees Gina.*]

EKDAL: Aye aye.

GINA: Do you want something, Grandad?

[*He goes in again. Gina lifts the basket.*]

GINA: Keep a sharp eye on him, make sure he doesn't go out.

HJALMAR: I will, yes. Listen, Gina, a bit of herring salad might do the trick. I dare say Relling and Holvik have been on the booze last night.

GINA: If they'd just give me enough time –

HJALMAR: Of course, take your good time.

GINA: I will, yes, and you can get a bit of work done –

HJALMAR: I am sitting here working. I work all I can.

GINA: Then you'll have so much finished, won't you?

[*She goes into the kitchen with the basket. Hjalmar sits working, slowly, reluctantly, on the photograph with a brush. Old Ekdal peeps in, looks round the studio and whispers.*]

EKDAL: Are you hard at it?

HJALMAR: I am, working hard on these photographs –

EKDAL: You are, God spare us. You're very busy. Indeed. Aye aye.

[*He goes in again, leaving the door open. For a moment Hjalmar works in silence, then puts down the brush and goes across to the door.*]

HJALMAR: Father, are you busy?

[*Ekdal mutters in the room.*]

EKDAL: If you're busy, so I'm busy. Aye.

HJALMAR: All right then.

[*He goes back to work again. Soon after, Ekdal appears in the doorway.*]

EKDAL: Hjalmar, I'm not that very busy.

HJALMAR: I thought you were writing.

EKDAL: The devil take Graberg, can't he wait a day or two? He won't die waiting.

HJALMAR: And you're not some kind of slave either.

EKDAL: And there is this other matter –

HJALMAR: Exactly, do you want me in there? Do you need a hand?

EKDAL: That might be a help.

[Hjalmar gets up.]

HJALMAR: Then we would have that finished.

EKDAL: We would. It needs to be finished by tomorrow. It is tomorrow, yes?

HJALMAR: It is tomorrow indeed.

[Hjalmar and Ekdal each slide a door inside. The morning sun shines through the skylight. A few pigeons fly to and fro, others sit cooing on the rafters. Now and then the clucking of hens comes from further back in the loft.]

HJALMAR: Go ahead, Father.

EKDAL: Are you not coming in?

HJALMAR: Yes, you know that – I might as well –

[He sees Gina in the kitchen door.]

HJALMAR: No, I've no time – I have to work – Now this mechanism –

[He pulls a cord which lets down a curtain, the lower part of which consists of a strip of old sail-cloth. The upper part is a piece of fishing net, stretched taut. The loft floor is no longer seen. Hjalmar goes across to the table.]

HJALMAR: There now, I can sit in peace for a while.

GINA: Is he fiddling about in there again?

HJALMAR: Would you prefer him down in Madam Eriksen's?

[He sits down.]

HJALMAR: Is there something you want? You were saying –

GINA: I only wanted to ask if we should serve lunch in here.

HJALMAR: Yes, but nobody's arrived so early yet, have they?

GINA: No, but I'm expecting the couple who want their photograph taken together.

HJALMAR: Damn them, let them have it taken another day.

GINA: No, darling, I've booked them after lunch, when you'll have your sleep.

HJALMAR: All right then. We'll eat in here.

GINA: Right. There's no rush to set the table. You can use it a while longer.

HJALMAR: I'm sitting here using the table all I can – do you see that?

GINA: Then you'll be free later on – do you see that?

[She goes into the kitchen. There is a brief pause. Inside the net, Ekdal calls from the loft door.]

EKDAL: Hjalmar.

HJALMAR: What?

EKDAL: Afraid we'll have to move the water-trough after all.

HJALMAR: I've been saying that the whole time.

EKDAL: Aye – aye – aye.

[He goes away from the door again. Hjalmar works a little while, glances towards the loft, half rises. Hedvig comes in from the kitchen. Hjalmar sits down quickly.]

HJALMAR: What do you want?

HEDVIG: I only wanted to be with you, Daddy.

[There is a short pause.]

HJALMAR: I think you're snooping – are you supposed to be spying on me?

HEDVIG: I am not.

HJALMAR: What's your mother doing out there?

HEDVIG: She's in the middle of making the herring salad.

[She goes over to the table.]

HEDVIG: Isn't there some little thing I could help you with, Daddy?

HJALMAR: No – it's best I work on my own – for as long as my strength is up to it. We'll all manage, Hedvig, as long as your father's health lasts –

HEDVIG: Stop, Daddy – don't say horrible things.

[She wanders about a little, stops by the sliding doors and looks into the loft.]

HJALMAR: What is he up to, Hedvig?

HEDVIG: I think he is making a new path up to the water trough.

HJALMAR: He'll never manage that on his own. And I'm doomed to sit here.

[Hedvig goes across to him.]

HEDVIG: Give me the brush, Daddy, I can do it, you'll see.

HJALMAR: Silly talk – you'll only ruin your eyes.

HEDVIG: I won't – give me the brush.

[Hjalmar gets up.]

HJALMAR: Well, it would only take a minute or two.

HEDVIG: So, what harm can it do?

[She takes the brush.]

HEDVIG: Right.

[She sits down.]

HEDVIG: And I have one here to use as a copy.

HJALMAR: Now don't hurt your eyes – do you hear me? I take no responsibility, it's all up to you, I'm telling you that.

[Hedvig continues retouching.]

HEDVIG: Yes, I'm listening.

HJALMAR: You're very clever, Hedvig. Just for a few minutes, you understand.

[He slips under the curtain into the loft. Hedvig sits at her work. Hjalmar and Ekdal are heard arguing inside. Hjalmar comes up to the net.]

HJALMAR: Hedvig, reach me those pliers – they're on the shelf. And that chisel.

[He turns back to the loft.]

HJALMAR: Now, Father, you'll see – please allow me to show you what I mean.

[Hedvig has got the tools from the shelf and hands them to him.]

HJALMAR: Thank you. Now it's just as well I came in.

[He goes away from the opening. They hammer away and joke together. Hedvig stands watching them. A moment later someone knocks at the hall door. She does not notice. Bareheaded and without an overcoat, Gregers Werle comes in and stands by the door.]

GREGERS: Hello.

[She turns and goes towards him.]

HEDVIG: Good morning. Please come in.

GREGERS: Thanks.

[He looks towards the loft.]

GREGERS: Do you have workmen in the house?

HEDVIG: No – it's Father and Grandfather. I'll tell them you're here.

GREGERS: No, don't – I'd prefer to wait a little.

[He sits on the sofa.]

HEDVIG: A bit of a mess –

[She is about to clear away the photographs.]

GREGERS: Leave them. Are these photographs waiting to be finished?

HEDVIG: Yes, I was just going to give Daddy a bit of help –

GREGERS: Don't let me disturb you.

HEDVIG: No.

[She moves the things over to her and starts to work. Gregers watches her in silence.]

GREGERS: Did the wild duck sleep well last night?

HEDVIG: It certainly did, thank you.

[He turns towards the loft.]

GREGERS: In the daytime it looks quite different than it did last in the moonlight.

HEDVIG: Yes, very different. It changes from the morning to the afternoon, and when it rains it doesn't look the same as it does in good weather.

GREGERS: Have you noticed that?

HEDVIG: I can see that, yes.

GREGERS: Do you like to be in there with the wild duck?

HEDVIG: I do, whenever it's possible –

GREGERS: But you don't have that much free time. You must go to school.

HEDVIG: Not any more. No. Daddy is afraid I'll ruin my eyes.

GREGERS: So he must read with you himself.

HEDVIG: Daddy's promised he will read with me. He's not got time yet.

GREGERS: Is there no-one else to help you?

HEDVIG: Yes, Mr Molvik – he's got a degree – but he's not the most dependable –

GREGERS: He's a drunk?

HEDVIG: He is indeed.

GREGERS: So you do have time for other things. And in there, there is a world all by itself, am I right?

HEDVIG: All by itself. And it's full of strange things.

GREGERS: Is it?

HEDVIG: It is. Large cupboards with books in them. And there's pictures in a lot of the books.

GREGERS: Really.

HEDVIG: And there's an old desk with drawers and flaps, and a big clock with figures that are meant to slide out, but the clock doesn't work anymore.

GREGERS: Time's ground to a halt in them – with the wild duck.

HEDVIG: It has. And there's old paint-boxes and stuff like that. And all the books as well.

GREGERS: And I suppose you read these books?

HEDVIG: Yes, when I'm able to. Most of them are in English though, I don't understand that. There's a really big book called Harryson's *History of London*. It's supposed to be a hundred years old. It's full of pictures. On the front of it is a picture of Death with an hourglass and a young girl. I think it's awful. But there are other pictures of churches and castles and streets and big ships sailing the sea.

GREGERS: Tell me where you got all these strange things.

HEDVIG: An old sea captain lived here once. He took them home. They called him 'The Flying Dutchman'! Now that was strange, because he wasn't Dutch.

GREGERS: He wasn't?

HEDVIG: No. But in the end he never returned and all this was left here.

GREGERS: Tell me this – when you're sitting in there looking at the pictures, don't you want to go and look at the great big world out there?

HEDVIG: Not at all. I'll always be at home helping my father and mother.

GREGERS: Retouching photographs?

HEDVIG: Not just that. I'd love to learn to engrave pictures like the ones in the English books.

GREGERS: Would you – what does your father say to that?

HEDVIG: I don't think Daddy likes it. Daddy's odd about things like that. He just talks about me learning to make baskets and weave straw. Imagine that. I see no point in that.

GREGERS: Not me either.

HEDVIG: Daddy is right though, if I'd learnt to weave baskets, I could have made the new one for the wild duck.

GREGERS: You could have, and no better person to do it.

HEDVIG: Yes, it's for my wild duck.

GREGERS: It is.

HEDVIG: I do own it. Daddy and Grandad can borrow it though, as often as they want.

GREGERS: What do they want with it?

HEDVIG: They look after it and build things for it – stuff like that.

GREGERS: Of course – the wild duck is the most wonderful creature in there.

HEDVIG: She is. She really is a wild bird. And it's so sad. Poor thing, she's all on her own.

GREGERS: Nobody belonging to her, like the rabbits –

HEDVIG: Nobody. Many of the hens, they've all been chicks together. But she has come so far away from all like her. That's why she is wonderful, the wild duck. No-one knows her. No-one knows where she's from either.

GREGERS: And she's been swept from the floor of the ocean.

[*Hedvig glances quickly at him, suppresses a smile and asks*]

HEDVIG: Why do you say the floor of the ocean?

GREGERS: What should I have said?

HEDVIG: You could say the bottom of the sea – or the sea bed.

GREGERS: I could just as well say the floor of the ocean.

HEDVIG: To me that sounds so strange, when I hear people say the floor of the ocean.

GREGERS: Why's that – tell me.

HEDVIG: No, I won't – it's stupid.

GREGERS: It's not – tell me why you've just smiled.

HEDVIG: It's just that – when it hits me out of the blue – when I think of everything in there – the whole room and all the things in there – I think it should be called the floor of the ocean. But that's stupid of course.

GREGERS: You shouldn't say that.

HEDVIG: It's only a loft.

[*He looks firmly at her.*]

GREGERS: Are you certain about that?

[*She is astonished.*]

HEDVIG: That it's a loft?

GREGERS: Yes, do you know that for certain?

[*Hedvig looks at him with an open mouth. Gina comes with a table cloth from the kitchen.*]

Lost Futures: Sebastian Barry's *Our Lady of Sligo*

ROY FOSTER

'Ireland, where is that country? Where are those lives that lay in store for us, in store like rich warm grain?' Jack and Mai O'Hara, Sebastian Barry's protagonists in his new play *Our Lady of Sligo*, bear witness to the forgotten Irish middle class just after independence. Their disorientation is not that of Thomas Dunne in *The Steward of Christendom* – the confused old Dublin Metropolitan Police Superintendent who did the British state in Ireland some service and has never quite understood why it has not been requited. The O'Haras are the Catholic bourgeoisie of the last Home Rule generation, born to inherit a world destroyed by the Sinn Féin revolution which began with the 1916 Rising and culminated in the 1921 Treaty. But like Thomas Dunne, or the wandering hero in Barry's novel *The Whereabouts of Eneas MacNulty*, they feel the future was robbed from them. Immobilised in the terrible present, they try to make sense of their past, disabled by forever rehearsing unfulfilled expectations.

Barry writes history plays in a special sense. *Our Lady of Sligo* is the sixth in the series which began with *Boss Grady's Boys*, and continued through *Prayers of Sherkin*, *White Woman Street*, and *The Only True History of Lizzie Finn* to *The Steward of Christendom*. His project is one of recovery – stitching back into the torn fabric of Irish history the anomalous figures from an extended Irish family. Mai and Jack have already appeared obliquely in *The Whereabouts of Eneas MacNulty*, glimpsed through windows and whispered about in their absence. Eneas knows 'there's some story there with the wife . . . as far as he's aware the wife is a very fine woman from Galway that Jack adores, whose father was quite the gentleman living out the Grattan Road; there's something else that no-one can tell him . . .' Later, the innocent Eneas hears about it; hears too that she has lost a child; thinks that marriage might be 'a sort of war with its own alarming injuries'. But the memory endures of secretly watching Jack reading to his daughter by lamplight: 'the child and the father and the book, here is the living scene more holy and sacred than any official ceremony, for which all wars are declared and every peace manufactured.'

Encountering Mai, Jack and Joanie twenty years later in *Our Lady of Sligo*, the war and injuries are more evident than the manufacture of peace. In plays and novel, the background to Barry's people is fighting, migration, revolution; their displacement is literal as well as psychological. Like Eneas, Mai Kirwin was born with the century; her assured background, the prosperous bourgeoisie of Galway, prepared her for a secure future which never came. The constitutional-nationalist Home Rule party, reunited under John Redmond in 1900, apparently exercised hegemony over Irish politics; from 1912 the enactment of Home Rule, and the restoration of an autonomous Irish parliament, seemed inevitable. Mai's palmy days as a student of Commerce at the university, however mythologised for personal purposes, reflect the reality of the times. Women had been graduating from the old Royal University since the 1890s, and the development of higher education for middle-class Catholic Irishwomen was boosted spectacularly by the National University legislation of 1908. This brought the Galway college into the new National University, and simultaneously gave a much fuller role to women in college life. The process mirrored the way Catholics had come to dominate most of the old bastions of Ascendancy privilege – in the legal profession, the world of medicine, the civil service, they decisively outnumbered Protestants.

However, the astonishing upheavals of the Irish revolution erased the optimism of the pre-war era, and the confidence of the old Redmondite world. Radical nationalists would traduce this class as 'shoneens', 'West Britons', or 'Castle Catholics', and accuse them of being 'anti-national'; the point was rather that their nationalism was of a different kind, and they nonetheless expected to take over the country through what the writer Tom Kettle (a standard-bearer for his National University generation) called the 'biped policy' of Home Rule – marching on one Irish and one imperial foot. The Sinn Féin revolution, and the efforts of the IRA under Michael Collins, would be directed just as much against this class as against the British. This is why the memoirs of the Irish doctor Patrick Heffernan, written in 1958, lament 'the heyday of the middle classes before the modern revolution came'. The new Free State wrote the *ci-devant* Catholic bourgeoisie out of its history, along with the Ascendancy elite they had been poised to replace. Yeats's notional 'dream of the noble and the beggarman', an Ireland without intermediate classes or confused allegiances, suited the purposes of nationalist state-builders as well as romantic idealists.

Mai and her husband sustain a different memory and tell a different story. Jack, from a humbler background than his wife, nonetheless gentrified himself through the traditional route of the British services: old Nigeria hand, British Army major, engineer, Fellow of the Royal Geological Society. As Mai details it with cruel accuracy, he modelled himself on the local upper-class Protestants:

> and by the time he did that, those people were all gone, or sunken back into a different life, and all their sons or many of them killed in the Great War, and their position destroyed by independence in the country generally. Jack tried to turn himself into a sort of British gentleman and by the time he achieved it, death and independence had erased his template. He was a weird creation in his own country. There were no posh Protestants left in Sligo to notice the Catholic butterfly painfully emerged from the dank caterpillar he had been. They couldn't greet him in the street, toff to toff, as he desired and longed for, because they no longer existed. It probably broke his heart just as much as marrying me did.

'Death and independence' are closely bound together in the existence rehearsed by Mai from her bed in Jervis Street nursing-home: like Winnie in Beckett's *Happy Days* or Momo in Murphy's *Bailegangaire*, she is a trapped woman constructing a narrative of her life. But she possesses nothing as sustaining as Winnie's handbag – or Winnie's self-deception. Instead, things are buried – Joanie's disastrous cake, the Kirwin statue in the Galway chapel, bodies in distant Africa. And, in every case, dug up again. The deaths of children, the demons of alcoholism, a secret history of shame, lies behind and around the history of a disappointment that is the disappointment of a whole class. The Ireland that they expected, the lives they wanted, remain like the dead Cissie and Colin: unbearable recollections of beings never brought to maturity.

The class which Mai comes from, and Jack achieves too late, cannot accept the Ireland that painfully struggled into being after the revolution and subsequent civil war: an Ireland where Jack and other employees of the British services have to surreptitiously change out of their uniforms on the returning mailboat, and which has no room for Mai's fine provincial style: '. . . a dress made by Mrs Ursula Doyle on Main Street to a French design. I know there was truth in that because we found the dress together in *TidBits*, as worn by Mrs Gary Cooper. A French dress by way of Paris by way of Hollywood by way of Sligo. A sort of translated dress, like an Irish song at school.'

In *The Steward of Christendom*, Thomas Dunne's daughter Annie makes a bitter prophecy in 1922, as her father prepares to hand over his authority to the new regime: 'It will be whins and waste everywhere, with bits of stones sticking up that were once Parliament, Castle and Cathedral. And people going round like scarecrows and worse . . . The like of Collins and his murdering men won't hold this place together. They haven't the grace or the style for it. So you needn't mourn your shops and hats and haircuts – they won't be there.' Ironically, and too late, it is exactly Collins's 'grace and style' which impress the outgoing Superintendent: but Collins is soon dead. The ideology of the new Ireland, especially after de Valera achieves ascendancy in the 1930s, imposes an Irish ideal which is both rural and frugal: Jack and Mai are ostentatiously neither. Shops and hats and haircuts may mean too much to them, but there is more to their vanished future than that. Fine Gael, the post-revolutionary party which might eventually express their aspirations and identifications, is considered 'cleaner' than de Valera's Fianna Fáil; but it is Jack's smart brother who makes a career as a local politician.

Still, for the O'Haras, the temporary refuge of late-colonial Africa, American sedans and big bungalows, does not answer. They are Irish, they come home. And alcohol, as too often in Ireland, presides inexorably over decline: Jack 'drinks a house' away, while drunkenness makes Mai see herself, with horror and self-hatred, as a changeling: on a visit to the country, she discovers an ancient country fear. 'I knew by first light that Mai Kirwin was not lying in that comfortable old bed, that country bed with its country linen and bedspread stitched by some forgotten old aunt, and the cock rousing everything in the stew of morning outside. I knew that lying in the bed was only the demon I had become.' By the 1950s, contrary to Annie Dunne's expectations, the new Irish middle class has been 'made': but the O'Haras have not been part of the process. Like many of their generation, they cannot quite believe what has become of them. The recurring images of a lost *douceur de vivre* – moths, moonlight, the corrugated iron dancehall by the sea, tennis-parties in darkening gardens – cannot prettify any of this, nor disguise the self-centredness that has dominated their unfulfilled lives.

Yet Barry's gallery of doomed and outlandish people, throughout his plays and fiction, sustain their own bursts of magificence. As Fintan O'Toole has pointed out, they are touched with grace, and never more so than in this play. If Mai is bitterly described by her daughter as 'Mammy of the gaps', she can also bring together the disconnected and suppressed parts of her story. As in so much of Barry's work, acceptance and redemption comes through the transfiguring power of memory, pouring in with the waves of language, unlocking the calcification of time – like the silted-up Garravogue river, waiting for the tide, which so obsesses Mai in Sligo. And their dead return to them, thoughtfully visiting, like Thomas Dunne's son (killed, with Tom Kettle, on the Western Front) in *The Steward of Christendom*. There is the memory of a child washed in a basin, remembered and replicated in a hospital bedroom; flowers magically appear at a moment of 'dark thoughts'; the possibility of love is at once obdurate and surprising, 'the ring in the brack'. In Barry's work as in Mai's narrative, mordant Irish humour and hard Irish truths are embedded in vertiginous sweeps of language. This dramatic verve locks *Our Lady of Sligo* into his wider enterprise of reclamation. Those same gifts of poetry, daring and breadth of emotion place Barry's plays firmly in the tradition of Synge and O'Casey. History, national as well as personal, is illuminated by the searchlight of a tragic imagination.

Cartographic Connections: Problems of Representation in Calypso Theatre Company's *The Business of Blood*

VIC MERRIMAN

Calypso Theatre Company is based in Dublin and has an administrative base in Glasgow. Its 1995 Mission Statement proposed:

> Calypso's mission is simple, practical and humble. We want to change the world . . . the change we want to effect is small, significant and possible . . . By our future world family, we will be remembered in one of two ways. We will either have been caring guardians who nurtured their inheritance – social, political, artistic, environmental and sacred – or we will have been the parasites who depleted some of the hope and possibility from their lives. We are all world citizens. Some of us are lucky enough to have inherited life saving rights, life enhancing social opportunities and life affirming creative possibilities. With those rights and privileges comes a responsibility to defend them for ourselves and for others.[1]

This amounts to an intention to produce theatre as an intervention in contemporary political and civil life, and to envisage in a new way, the world as a stage, or site of contestation of choices made in the political sphere. Calypso's declared objectives include social change through ethical questioning of the dominant, and dialogue with the voiceless in order to bring their stories from the margins to the centre of public concern. The wager is that as exploitation is revealed as a root cause of the plight of such peoples, their oppression as a function of the political economy of the West will be exposed, interrogated and changed by popular pressure. In this, the Calypso project positions itself among current tendencies in cultural criticism, postcolonial writing and the practices of twentieth-century oppositional theatre.

Calypso's first production was Donal O'Kelly's *Hughie on the Wires* (1993), which placed a young Derry man in El Salvador. O'Kelly's

Trickledown Town (1994) was set on a Caribbean island state, and employed pointed farce to address the activities of the World Bank and their local consequences in a rundown urban area. In 1995 Calypso presented and toured *The Business of Blood* by Donal O'Kelly and Kenneth Glenaan. This play stages the story of Chris Cole, a Christian pacifist, who broke into BAe Stevenage and damaged components of Hawk jetfighters, in order to draw attention both to their use against civilian populations in East Timor and what he saw as the hypocrisy of a British government which publicly stated that it did not sell arms to regimes known to be involved in human rights abuses. Cole remained in the building after his assault, in order to facilitate his arrest.

> CHRIS: I've never met anyone in prison who could get their heads around this part. It's called taking responsibility for your actions. I've done this. But I'm not a criminal. British Aerospace are the criminals.[2]

Calypso's decision to stage Cole's story comes as no surprise. *The Business of Blood* is an exercise in cultural remapping from a counter-hegemonic position, an attempt at reshaping the geopolitical coordinates which define North-South relations. Those relations produce practices of representation which erase injustice and enable exploitation of indigenous populations in the eastern and southern hemispheres.

Benedict Anderson draws attention to the role of the map in the extension of imperialist control, political and ideological. In exposing 'the alignment (war by war, treaty by treaty) of map and power'[3] he identifies mapping as a culturally formative representational practice, itself the result of conceptualisation as much as conquest. Once established, the map exerts a telling influence on the conceptualisation of subsequent political relations and power struggles, both intranational and international:

> the map-as-logo . . . In its final form all explanatory glosses could be summarily removed: lines of longitude and latitude, place names, signs for rivers, seas and mountains, neighbours. Pure sign, no longer compass to the world. In this shape, the map entered an infinitely reproducible series . . . Instantly recognisable, everywhere visible, the logo-map penetrated deep into the popular imagination, forming a powerful emblem for the anti-colonial nationalisms being born.[4]

According to Anderson, the terrain involved in the practices and consequences of mapping is as much an imaginary as a geographical location. He makes it plain that certain practical consequences for human relations follow from this:

> Since 1963 there have been many bloody episodes in West New Guinea ... but these brutalities pale by comparison with Jakarta's savagery in ex-Portugueuse East Timor, where in the first three years after the 1976 invasion an estimated one-third of the population of 600,000 died from war, famine, disease and 'resettlement'. I do not think it a mistake to suggest that the difference derives in part from East Timor's absence from the logos of the Netherlands East Indies and, until 1976, of Indonesia's.[5]

The consequences of falling outside the perimeter of metropolitan consciousness are stark and final.[6] In the case of *The Business of Blood*, this insight represents the point of entry to the struggle over meaning, power and human possibility which characterises the postmodern moment. Calypso's attempt is to refigure the audience as students of contemporary political culture along the lines suggested by Ben Agger:

> Cultural studies emphasises that culture is conflict over meaning – over how to assign value to human existence, expression, experience.[7]

The play is positioned as a cultural document, composed of a variety of apparently unconnected, but actually intimate events. It is in the articulation of those events that remapping is made possible.

The necessity for such a corrective project is forcefully underpinned by Anderson's argument. How does it sit with influential assumptions and expectations of contemporary Irish theatre? *The Business of Blood* provoked a deal of argument over its status in the columns of the *Irish Times*. It was dismissed in David Nowlan's review as follows:

> ... it has been said, inter alia, that drama is comprised of conflict and change, yet within this work there is no dramatic conflict and there has been no significant change at its conclusion. This is theatre being used to make a point rather than a point being used to create drama.[8]

The message is clear, this is not dramatic art. Fintan O'Toole responded:

> There is a strong tendency to patronise such writing, to see it as at best a lesser form of art, at worst a corruption of aesthetic purity ... The question posed by *The Business of Blood* – whether civilisation can be said to exist at all while complicity with mass murder is treated as a legitimate business – is a question that addresses the very possibility of art itself.[9]

It is clear that when contemporary Irish theatre begins to address the terrain of geopolitics it opens up the question of its own topography as well. In defending, even championing this play, O'Toole argues for the expansion of the domain of art, the extension of its borders to include this play:

> There has to be room in the theatre for work as instructive, as angry and as well aimed as this.[10]

The critical reception of the play is of considerable interest, and an analysis of its content would yield a rich account of the underpinnings of a range of discourses active in popular debates in art, politics and economics. One of the problems associated with art as closed, transcendent category is its received status as essentially unconcerned with the struggles of contemporary living, except insofar as such struggles are perceived and expressed by the artist as a kind of turmoil out of which s/he must create order. A historicised, culturally critical perspective is presented as the domain of politics or social science. Art and social praxis are mutually exclusive. In this sense, *The Business of Blood* can only be received as an ungainly hybrid or as a distant relative for whom space must be made, however much of an affront its presence constitutes to the rest of the family. The narrowness of this response points to the urgency of the need to address received ways of thinking about theatre and society. What is needed is a radical repositioning of art, an acknowledgement of its thorough implication in the social order. No enlargement of the sealed category itself will enable cultural production to interact with social reality.

Art refigured as one mode of cultural production among many, a site bounded by politics, economics, pedagogy – each with mutually porous borders – provides a critical structure which can begin to address the totality of the play as project. Cornel West announces this as a postmodern imperative to enable human agency:

> . . . a new kind of cultural worker is in the making, associated with a new politics of difference . . . [whose distinctive features include a commitment] to historicize, contextualize and pluralize by highlighting the contingent, provisional, variable, tentative, shifting and changing . . . [W]hat makes [this commitment] novel – along with the cultural politics [it] produce[s] – is how and what constitutes difference, the weight and gravity it is given in representation, and the way in which highlighting issues like exterminism, empire, class, race, gender, sexual orientation, age, nation, nature and region, at this historical moment acknowledges some discontinuity and disruption from previous forms of cultural critique.[11]

It is within such a frame of reference that *The Business of Blood*, a manifestation of the Calypso project, begins to make sense and becomes itself available for critique. Postmodern and postcolonial cultural practices envisage a reinvention of egalitarian democracy by means of a radical rethinking of human agency. It is necessary to ask to what extent this play enables the critical analysis necessary to the development of cultural praxis.

The Business of Blood addresses the unfinished project of the European Enlightenment – civil equality. It does so, however on the global stage provided by the conjunction of postmodernity and postcolonialism. No dialogue in which the colonised subject is either spoken for or is expected to speak can ignore the historical disequilibrium which haunts any attempt to initiate such a conversation. Spivak exposes the central ethical problem confronting those who would speak for 'the subaltern':

> According to Foucault and Deleuze [in the First World, under the standardization and regimentation of socialized capital, though they do not seem to recognize this] . . . the oppressed can speak and know their conditions. We must now confront the following question: On the other side of the international division of labour from socialized capital, inside and outside the circuit of the epistemic violence of imperialist law and education supplementing an earlier economic text, can the subaltern speak?[12]

In this play, Calypso speaks to metropolitan audiences in the (erased) names of those on the margins of terrain mapped and administered in the interests of dominant economic and political interests. This involves the company in the representation of the oppressed. Spivak warns against the influence of 'the semiosis of the social text [in which] . . . "the peasant" is marked only as a pointer to an irretrievable consciousness'.[13] As the 'effaced itinerary of the subaltern subject'[14] is relocated from the geographical context of East Timor to the contested sites of Western political economy, the danger of compounding physical violence in history with epistemic violence in representation is all too present. In the process of relocation, the voice of the subaltern, already barely audible among the edifices of Western and neo-colonial political landscapes, is effectively erased as an account of the actuality it is said to speak.

The play's structure is a montage assembled from Chris Cole's actual actions against BAe, his trials and hearings before the courts, his encounters with the company's rationale and with the police investigation into his crimes. Interwoven into this documentary narrative is a stylised account of the massacre of civilians in Dili, East Timor, by invading Indonesian paratroops. The play's content emerges in the deft juxtaposition of document and stylised representation. The intention is to expose the moral bankruptcy of BAe by linking Cole's action to its context in a cause–effect relation. In this way, the play lays down its stake in the wager mentioned above. The leap of faith involved in the placing of the bet turns on a conception of the Western audience as susceptible to change based on argument structured around passion and fact. The frame of reference for this is demonstrably, and necessarily European. Change will result from a sense of outrage at European complicity in the inhumane treatment of its others. That is what the play will stage. What it will not stage is any change in the possibility of reading the other differently, of the other as potential agent.

The play does stage two individual case studies of Timorese experience of state terror: one female and one male. In both cases, CHRIS (Cole *represented*) stands centre stage and recites verse in which the personal history is reflected upon and offered both as evidence of Cole's *actual* commitment and as a dramatic device to link to human experience the abstractions and statistics which dominate the documentary content. CHRIS becomes a metaphor for the kind of principled re-mapping in which Calypso assert they are engaged.

The Poem to Abel Araujo is recited as the context for Cole's decision to break an injunction restraining him from entering BAe property.

> CHRIS: On November 12, 1994 the third anniversary of the day Indonesian soldiers opened fire on a crowd in Dili – five hundred killed, I went to BAe Stevenage. I published a leaflet calling for a mass trespass. I walked in the gates.
>
> [*Silence. Chris stands. While he recites the poem to Abel Araujo, he burns a piece of paper with Abel Araujo's name on it.*]

No Hawks in Dili massacre
let's be clear
but the men who ordered it
are kept in place by the power they glean
from the greasy palm
that gives them the tools
so willingly
to carve you into stone
Abel Araujo.

Here lie cinders
dust of your name
on the patch of earth
British Aerospace
absurdly say they own
to reproduce the moment
when you smiled
or sang or just sat there,
before –

Abel Araujo, we remember you.
Vitally. [15]

Cole as metaphor is also present in CHRIS as self-knowing subject, consciously and deliberately entering history. Abel Araujo is registered as a poignant absence, whose entry into history is occasioned by his death. His death is itself only significant in its relationship to Cole's decision to become a witness to, and on behalf of a people on the margins of European consciousness. Abel Araujo's presence in history is as a fixed point defined by its inability to make history. The paradox is fully exposed in this moment of representation, when CHRIS stages the actual Cole in the act of bearing witness – vitally – to a representation of Abel Araujo, victim, dead. Spivak's subaltern position is staged as that presence which is always already an absence. The European presence includes, interprets and exhausts the Asian absence. If the subaltern cannot speak, this moment demonstrates that the metropolitan cannot speak the subaltern position without staging its negation. The gesture performed by CHRIS amounts to a decolonising which is actually a conclusive colonisation of Araujo by Cole. Trapped in the iconography of liberal guilt, the subaltern victim is figured as incapable of independent existence, not to mention the agency necessary to participate in a reinvention of democracy on a global scale.

Calypso commit themselves to achievable social change. They propose to engage with the actual world, with possible worlds in prospect. Accordingly, they are obliged to begin with existing maps. They are faced with the task of developing new forms, not conjuring them from within their own transcendent consciousness. In important ways, the new maps will be developments from, even functions of the old ones.

> the role of cartography . . . in post-colonial writing in general, cannot be solely envisaged as the reworking of a particular spatial paradigm, but consists rather in the implementation of a series of creative revisions which register the transition from a colonial framework within which the writer is compelled to recreate and reflect upon the restrictions of colonial space to a post-colonial one within which he or she acquires the freedom to engage in a series of 'territorial disputes' which implicitly or explicitly acknowledge the relativity of modes of spatial (and, by extension, cultural) perception.[16]

In similar fashion, the search for theatrical aesthetics which include the possibility of liberation while staging the actuality of oppression begins with existing forms. The burning of the name on paper symbolises an act of cremation which, as a ritual dramatic action familiar to both Eastern and Western spirituality is itself an affirmation of a life to come. Cole's ritual scattering in England of the ashes of Abel Araujo's name goes to the heart of the geopolitical remapping which Calypso regard as the goal and purpose of contemporary cultural production for social change.

The actual gesture performs multiple functions. At the level of propaganda it transforms BAe Stevenage into a cemetery, a place of death. At the level of ethics, it achieves the recoding of the plant as 'a patch of earth'. In so doing it problematises the laws under which Cole was actually restrained from trespass. More significantly, it asserts, in what Huggan refers to as a 'cartographic connection', the identity of value between the earth upon which the imaginary 'Britain' has been constituted as democratic homeland and that on which the actual East Timor has become a tyrannised necropolis. By this means is remapping initiated in a problematic theatrical gesture which is also a radical statement. The dramatic metaphor embodied in the same content critiqued above, simultaneously opens up the ethical necessity for disidentification with power relations deriving from colonial cartography. The audience is challenged to embrace the negotiation of a postmodern topography based on political rather than physical proximities.

> Too often art and artists travel a journey where the landscapes they move through and the people they encounter become mere observations, ideas to be used. Other artists travel as participants in their landscapes. Their work is about, and comes from their interaction with their fellow world citizens ... Our landscape covers the planet. Our family is global. Our creativity is a critical one.[17]

The Business of Blood is a valuable contribution to a dialogue based on a belief in social egalitarianism. It disturbs received constructs of geopolitical relations and inaugurates a critical project of participative travel through historically charged landscapes. The reading offered above intends to draw attention to the necessity that contemporary cultural workers engage with the detail of the representations they offer to their audiences. In the case of *The Business of Blood* this is important in representing the work's commitment to exposing the global reach and local implications of what Samir Amin calls 'actually existing capitalism'. It is even more crucially necessary to acknowledge the historically embedded but culturally active inscriptions of power in the acts of representation themselves. The lesson of *The Business of Blood* is clear. Cultural remapping positions cultural workers as producers of their own and others' places, where place includes sites positioned both geographically and in historical processes and power relations. In order that change through dialogical engagement and collective agency be brought into being, it is necessary that existing conditions be represented in such ways as facilitate their movement between the actual and the possible. Radical theatre practice must struggle for content within its own interpretive stances toward metaphors made in the light of existing conventions of representation.

Notes and References

1 *Calypso Theatre Company: Mission Statement* (Calypso Productions, 1995).
2 K. Glenaan and D. O'Kelly, *The Business of Blood* (unpublished Third Draft 1995), p. 14
3 B. Agger, *Cultural Studies as Critical Theory* (Falmer, 1992), p. 10.
4 B. Anderson, *Imagined Communities* (Verso, 1993), p. 173.
5 ibid., p. 177.
6 Calypso is certainly alive to the concrete significance of such conceptual erasures. See the booklet accompanying the play, *Information and Action on Arms*.
7 Agger, *Cultural Studies as Critical Theory*, p. 10.
8 D. Nowlan, 'Polemic driven to a foregone conclusion', *The Irish Times,* 15 September 1995.
9 F. O'Toole, 'Second Opinion: A powerful gesture', *The Irish Times,* 26 September 1995.
10 ibid.
11 C. West, 'The new cultural politics of difference', in R. Ferguson et al. (eds.), *Out There: Marginalisation and Contemporary Culture* (1993).
12 G.C. Spivak, 'Can the Subaltern Speak' in B. Ashcroft, G. Griffiths, H. Tiffin (eds.), *The Post-Colonial Studies Reader* (Routledge, 1995), p. 25.
13 ibid., p. 28.
14 ibid.
15 Glenaan and O'Kelly, *The Business of Blood*, p. 21.
16 G. Huggan, *Decolonizing the Map* in Ashcroft, 1995, pp. 410-411.
17 *Calypso Theatre Company: Mission Statement*, 1995.

1798: The Recurrence of Violence and Two Conceptualizations of History[1]

JOEP LEERSSEN

The violence and turmoil of 1798 made sense in one aspect only: its recurrent nature. It recalled, not only the French Revolution of 1789 and the Jacobite rising in Scotland in 1745, but also, most foregroundedly, the Ulster rising of 1641. What is more, in the decades before 1798 the Gaelic historical consciousness, as expressed in writings like those of Keating and Ó Rathaile, had begun to be transmitted to English-speaking Ireland. That historical awareness involved a strong sense of oppression and trauma, which in turn provided a sounding board for those nationally-minded commentators who saw the bleak public climate of the post-1798 decades as a re-enactment of the doomed failure of Irish national aspirations ever since Strongbow.

Once seen as a link in the chain of conflicts characterizing Irish history since the Middle Ages, 1798 therefore inspired nineteenth-century historical awareness in a twofold way: on the one hand, because people came to view conflict as a recurrent, normal mode for historical development, and on the other hand, because it fixed a sense that in Ireland such crises ended in attrition and defeat rather than in resolution. In this article, I want to argue that the one mode (which I will call 'the conflictual paradigm in historical consciousness'), with its idealistic and historicist implications, is shared by Ireland and by other European countries alike, while the other (which I will term 'the traumatic paradigm') marks Ireland rather as a subaltern, 'colonial' country.

European terms: the conflictual paradigm

. . . down the lampless darkness they came,
Moving like women: Justice, Truth, such figures
Thomas Kinsella, 'Another September'

Many historians have followed in the footsteps of Sir Richard Musgrave in pointing out that the 1798 rising was a re-enactment (of sorts) of the rising of 1641. This was not only a helpful comparison in order to understand the divisive and traumatic nature of that event; I think it marks a cardinal transition in Irish ways of viewing history. Revolutions, crises and civil wars had marked that history, but primarily as anomalous singularities, catastrophic points of aberration. After 1798 it appears as if a paradigm is established; violent episodes are a regular feature of Irish history, recurrent because they correspond to an underlying structure. A pattern emerges of tension, outburst, repression and renewed tension – a pattern which to students of Irish history nowadays seems the familiar hallmark of Irish history from Strongbow onwards, but which may only have begun to stand out in glaring obviousness when bewildered onlookers, who with Grattan's Parliament had looked forward to a benign 'End of History', Fukuyama-style, tried to make sense of the fresh turmoil. 1798 makes sense to the onlookers of the time if it is fitted into a pattern of other conflicts: 1641 in Ulster, 1745 in Scotland, 1789 in France. Indeed 1798 is the final clinching element which makes a collection of isolated episodes stand out as a series. Following 1789 and its Irish echo 1798, it becomes difficult to see history (especially Irish history) other than as a concatenation of revolts.

The traditionary view of history, as an incremental accumulation of the experience of causes and effects, with the polity floating like a ship downstream on the river of time, and with politics aimed at the avoidance and reparation of conflict and imbalance, becomes untenable. Burke's profound dismay at the French Revolution was not in the last place historiographical: the Revolution heralded a sense of history and politics where progress was predicated on conflict, driven by the energy of clashing social interests. To the extent that Burke advocates a sense of social harmony, he also advocates a vision of history as ideally tranquil and traditionary: community and tradition are two sides of the same conservative coin.

That point was well taken by one-nation Tories in Burke's wake, such as Disraeli in Britain and Samuel Ferguson in Ireland. Their ideal of resolving social conflict into a nationwide community is also an attempt to defuse that historical consciousness which thrives on remembered injustice. Ferguson's poetry celebrates a communitarian unity where all Irishmen concur in shared love of the Green Sod, each knowing his place in society, the humble peasant led by the benevolent paternalism of a Protestant élite. By the same token, that vision is nourished by a Burkean sense of consensual history; witness Ferguson's vehement rejection of Hardiman's *Irish Minstrelsy* commemorating the hatred and disaffection of the dispossessed Gaels of Penal days, as expressed in their Jacobite *aislingí*. For Ferguson, Hardiman's refusal to let bygones be bygones, and the fact that the *Irish Minstrelsy* serves to recall such anger after Emancipation, is as mischievous and destructive as Burke found the French Revolution's tendency to tender the unpaid bills of past centuries of injustice to the contemporary Church and nobility.

Once crises are seen as part of a series, as paradigmatic, as a recurrent and non-anomalous feature of history, then history presents itself as a seismic process, predicated on the normalcy of tensions which will accumulate until they break forth in violent conflict. I do not find much evidence for such a conceptualization of history before 1789, and I find it everywhere after 1798: in Ireland, to a lesser extent in Britain, and markedly present in Continental Germany and France.

In Ireland, we see it as a point where all the partisan historical writings of the period 1800–1830, no matter what their different ideological backgrounds, concur: Protestants like Musgrave, United Irishmen like Taaffe and Carey, or old Patriots like Curran and Barrington all in their way see 1798 as a fresh manifestation of long-contained discord within the Irish political system. Moore's *Captain Rock* goes as far as symbolizing this self-renewing pattern of 'English misrule and Irish rebellion' in a generational metaphor, by writing that tract in the form of a family novel of succeeding 'Rocks'. It is perhaps as a result of this paradigmatic shift in historical consciousness that so much history-writing reverts to the crude mode of partisan pamphleteering, forgetting the lessons of the 'philosophical' historiography of the Enlightenment, with its serene ideals of detachment, even-handedness and sceptical source-criticism. Most of the historical writings of the post-Union decades involve personal memoirs and personal narratives and indeed most fiction tends to follow the same pattern.[2] On the whole, 1798, for all that it was reflected upon and written about, seems to have been a cause for embarrassment and confusion, a symptom of the enduring and uncomfortable dividedness and fractiousness of Irish society and of Irish history.

There is a remarkable combination of attitudes: on the one hand, the 1798 rebellion (and Irish history and politics generally) became unmentionable almost, in a rictus of discreet 'don't mention the war' avoidance, while on the other hand there was much eloquent preoccupation with the painful topic. One may perhaps compare this contradictory reflex to the decades after the collapse of the Third Reich, which were (and still are) characterized everywhere by much soul-searching and by many historical accounts and testimonies (many of them, strangely, motivated by the fear that not enough was being done to remember the unique horror of it all), while all this remembrancing and account-taking has been accompanied by the widely-endorsed sense as formulated by Adorno that the intractable unspeakability of that horror forbade literary representation.

It is for a similar reason perhaps that John Kells Ingram's piece of verse in *The Nation* became so memorable: its opening line, 'Who fears to speak of ninety-eight?' hits the nail squarely on the head. In the mid-1840s 1798 was only beginning to become mentionable, beginning to be made accessible for positive commemoration and political inspiration, after an embarrassed and confused incubation period of half a century. Madden's and Maxwell's seminal historical accounts were published in these years, and the *Life of Theobald Wolfe Tone*, by his son William, saw its first Dublin publication (after previous ones in Washington and Paris). The symbolic, inspirational function of 1798 in Irish national thought dates from the mid-1840s, and it does so in a nationalist view of Irish history which is emphatically concerned with the fitful nature of the Irish past, and where the main value of each act of resistance is that it continues a tradition and inspires future rebels.

The conflictual view of history is slightly less predominant in England. Although it would be wrong to ignore the English radical tradition which continues from Godwin into Chartism, the Burkean paradigm managed, famously, to survive the Revolution's challenge. Thus, while Walter Scott's novels are often set in periods of conflict and national division, they always point to a harmonious resolution; their implied conservative ideal is that a happy end can be achieved consisting of purging the extremes, political conciliation and historical continuity. The only major voice to express the 'spasmodic' view is that of Carlyle, who saw history as a long struggle between willpower and chaos, and who chose, precisely, the French Revolution to celebrate that sublime and terrifying clash. Perhaps the deeper reason why Carlyle, though an intolerant bigot where Ireland was concerned, was so close to the hearts of the Young Irelanders, was that he expressed so powerfully a 'sublime', conflict-based, un-British and uncomplacent vision of history.[3] And it was perhaps also the deeper reason why O'Connell and the Young Irelanders proved incompatible allies: they belonged to different paradigms of viewing history, and O'Connell's politico-historical vision was closer to Burke than to Carlyle.

While Carlyle's interpretation of the French Revolution is an exemplification of the conflictual view of history, it is in itself an example of trends which were more widespread on the Continent; especially that of romantic Idealism. Everywhere in Carlyle the main historical actors are, not men and women or even groups of people, but abstract nouns written with a capital:

Order, Chaos, Conflict, Will. Behind the actual occurrences Carlyle sees transcendent forces and Platonic ideas at work. It is an idealist reflex which he shares with other romantic historians such as Michelet, who defined the French Revolution as *dans son principe le triomphe du droit, la résurrection de la justice, la réaction tardive de l'idée contre la force brutale.* The essence of human affairs lies in Ideas, in abstract principles; and to get to know them means truly *rerum cognoscere causas* and to apprehend the true nature of things.

Such romantic Idealism comes hand in glove with the conflict-based view of history such as it is applied by the likes of Carlyle and Michelet. The two are theoretically fused in the dialectical philosophy of Hegel, with its restless, Faustian, fugatically spiralling movement of thesis, antithesis and synthesis. Even Marx was to take over Hegel's dialectics, but chose to ground them in material, economic conditions rather than in the idealist abstractions of Hegelian *Geist* (as he put it: 'We must turn Hegel from his head back onto his feet'). But, regardless whether we trace Hegel's dialectical idealism or Marx's dialectical materialism, both are firmly children of the French Revolution in that, in their view, humankind's trajectory through time and history is propelled by the *primum movens* of confrontation.

In this sense, then, the legacy of 1798 in Irish historical thought is highly similar to the legacy of 1789 to Continental thought: a sense of history moving through the contractions and expansions of confrontation and resolution. Of course, there were few card-carrying Hegelians or Marxists active on the Irish intellectual scene (though a tentative filiation might be traced from Schelling to Michelet to Davis), but the parallel is so strong that in both cases we can see similar conditions lead to similar consequences. For the dialectical view of history led, both in Ireland and on the Continent, to a strong sense of historicism. By that term (which I use in the Popperian sense) I mean the idea that it must be possible to discern large-scale patterns in the vertiginous welter of historical conflict, and thence to infer predictions for the future course of political events.

Indeed, the conflict-based view of history is disconcerting in that it lacks the orderly sense of direction that the traditionary cause-and-effect model would have. At its worst, it might give rise to a sense of human affairs as an ungovernable maelstrom of confusion, chaos and random incident (as it would sometimes seem in the view of men like Schopenhauer or Nietzsche). The only safeguard against this threatening sense of random chaos is to presuppose that all the conflict and confusion is itself governed, at a deep, fundamental level, by some steering agency which gives the dialectical turmoil some direction, some sense of progress. Romantic Idealists in the tradition of Hegel and Michelet therefore often develop an almost mystical sense of 'historical necessity', of a vague 'Zeitgeist', of an abstract drive in the nature of things which establishes that for certain developments 'the time has come', while other patterns are somehow metaphysically doomed to oblivion because they have been bypassed by history (or History, to use the capitalization so dear to idealists like Carlyle).

In other words: the dialectical view of history requires an entelechy, a teleology, the idea that, for all the confrontations and conflicts, there is an essential direction into which history has to move. What is more, a proper understanding of history will enable us to foretell what this direction looks like; and that is 'historicism'. For Marxists, there is of course the 'historical necessity' of the Revolution, the uprising of the proletariat and the advent of a classless society. And in Ireland, the same teleological way of looking at a historical future was derived from the same dialectical way of analysing the past. 1798 gave rise to the nationalist perspective that every generation needed to reassert Ireland's right to independence, and the ultimate historical perspective of this apostolic succession of national champions was, of course, that of the country's sovereign autonomy. Much as 1789 ultimately inspired Marx and Lenin, so 1798 ultimately inspired Davis and Pearse; and in that respect, then, the legacy of 1798, placed as it was into a paradigm of serial revolts, gave rise to an Irish nationalism whose historical vision followed larger European patterns.

But there is another legacy of 1798 which is not so easily squared with metropolitan European trends, and which might instead be more fruitfully seen in 'colonial' terms.

Subaltern terms: the traumatic paradigm

I will dream it again
Thomas Kinsella, 'Wormwood'

Much of nineteenth-century historical culture is celebratory, 'monumental' as Nietzsche called it. The nineteenth century is the century of statues, monuments, feasts and centenaries, musea and celebrations. Ernest Renan, in his classic *Qu'est-ce qu'une nation* of 1881, sees this as one of the main bonding agents in achieving national solidarity: the 'awareness of having achieved great things together, and the will to do more'. The governments of the nation-states assiduously fostered this celebratory awareness by constantly invoking the great past, cultivating traditions or inventing them where necessary. In all the capitals and cities of Europe, national heroes are canonized and honoured by public monuments: Nelson on pillars in Sackville Street and Trafalgar Square, Boadicea on Westminster

Bridge, Vercingetorix in Clermont-Ferrand, Arminius in the Teutoburg Forest . . .

At the same time, however, Renan as famously pointed out that all this celebration of national glories was feasible only by disregarding the legacy of history's losers. Heroes are, after all, heroes by virtue of having beaten and silenced the competition, yet having obliterated their claims from the record. Thus, Renan warned, the progress of the historical sciences might bring facts to light which would testify to the injustice and intolerance at the heart of the nation state's success story, which might alert the more marginalized parts of the body politic to a historical sense of their grievances, and which as a result might have a disruptive effect on the celebratory propaganda of national unity.

Renan's prediction has been amply borne out since the time he made it. One of the great movements in twentieth-century history-writing and its historical consciousness is that our most sympathetic interest ought to go out, not to the laureled *campionissimi* of history, but to their victims, and that an enormous historical task lay in the project of giving the silenced losers of history their place in the historical record. The rural and urban poor of the early modern period; the heterodox peasantry with their folk beliefs and superstitions called before the Inquisition; women; slaves and workers: all these have been given a place on the historiographical agenda.

Indeed the emancipation of marginalized groups crucially involves the recuperation of a sense of history. This is self-evident since their marginalization consisted in large part of robbing them of their historical awareness in the first place. Women's emancipation required women's history; the emancipation of African Americans likewise necessitated the re-establishment of a historical sense, with cultural projects reaching from Alex Haley's *Roots* to the recent film *Amistad.*

Obviously, the recuperation of such subaltern histories could not follow the celebratory machismo of the metropolitan European monumental culture of nineteenth-century vintage. Instead, it appears as if the strongest sense of historical community consists, not of a sense of 'having achieved great things together', but rather of 'having endured great suffering together'. Thus, the second half of the twentieth century has witnessed the emergence of a new paradigm in historical consciousness which is based on remembered injustice and persecution rather than on victories and success stories. Jewish historical sense and collective identity rests on the shared trauma of the Shoah; African Americans derive their historical identity from the slave trade; and similar awareness of past grievance and injustice as the formative collective experience underlies other subaltern histories, from homosexuals to the former European colonies. This is now becoming known as the 'traumatic paradigm'.

When seen in this perspective, Irish historical consciousness after 1798 partakes of the 'traumatic paradigm', so characteristic of subaltern groups and cultures, rather than of the metropolitan, celebratory pattern. Indeed Ireland may well count as a harbinger of this paradigm. A sense of Irish history as a series of defeats, injustices and mortifications is not only to be found in the decades following 1798, but can even be traced back further, into the native tradition of eighteenth-century Gaelic Ireland. At least from Dáibhí Ó Bruadair and Aogán Ó Rathaile onwards, there is a lively and widespread sense that the Gaels are persecuted by their Godless opponents, who unleash every form of tyranny and iniquity on them. While this sense of history as oppression and grievance was originally (naturally) limited to the Gaelic underclass with its separate language, culture and aspirations, and unknown to the colonists and the authorities, the tentative cultural osmosis of the Patriotic decades after 1760 saw an increasing transmission of cultural material and attitudes from the Gaelic world to sympathetic Anglo-Irish antiquarians and literati, and an increasing participation of native scholars in the élite's intellectual life (albeit usually in the subordinate role of amanuensis, assistant, translator or scribe). As a result of these contacts, we see that among Patriots at least, a sense of 'national' Irish history begins to reach back beyond the Protestant interpretation of Ulster in 1641, interiorizes the Gaelic celebration of Irish antiquity and shares the Gaelic sense of tragedy at the fall of the native aristocracy and the ensuing colonial oppression.

If 1798 presents, in the overly flip formula, a confluence of Jacobite and Jacobin, then this is perhaps truest in the sense that the idea of history-as-oppression and as a series of tragic failures, so prominent in the Jacobite native tradition, passed into the Anglo-Irish nationalist conscience around this time. Once 1798 stood out as a doomed project, it could take its place, not only in the concatenation of violent ethnic conflicts, but also in the tradition of tragic failures followed by bleak oppression. Moore's *Captain Rock* draws on historical interpretations which come straight from Keating and which are redolent of the Hidden Ireland, and which would not have been available to him except through the cross-cultural transmission that had taken place in the later decades of the eighteenth century, from Charles O'Conor to Theophilus O'Flanagan; Hardiman's *Irish Minstrelsy* likewise transmits this Gaelic sense of history as a long torment of iniquity from the hermetic compliance of the native tradition into the literate culture of urban Anglo-Ireland.

In other words, Ireland is in the unique position of salvaging a native, literate voice of outrage and anger, almost silenced and locked into the secret hermeticism of its oppressed language, and affording it a platform in the language of the dominant culture. As a result, Anglo-Irish nationalism can incorporate and interiorize that subaltern sense of historical trauma which was to find its voice elsewhere only much later. For many Irish onlookers after 1798, Irish history is a nightmare. It was said by Gerald Griffin and by Joyce's Stephen Dedalus; a sense of history as a nightmarish burden of uncanny familiarity, repeating the dreary pattern of revolt and defeat over and over again, as in a neurosis or a nightmare, has been evinced by the tradition of Irish gothic which reaches from Maturin to Le Fanu to Kinsella; and the entire nineteenth century is obsessed by the idea that history in this country no longer progresses, but has become stuck like a needle in the groove of past recrimination and the burden of old blood and guilt. All this is a far cry from the Macaulays, Michelets and Treitschkes elsewhere in Europe at the time.

Ireland, then, as it reels from the shock of 1798, partakes both of European metropolitan patterns in nineteenth-century historical consciousness and of a 'third world', 'colonial', subaltern historical consciousness. That in itself is an indication that the much debated question whether Ireland is a first- or a third-world country, a mainstream Europan nation-state or an ex-colony, should not be put in stringent either-or terms. The most exciting challenge for future historians might lie, rather, in studying the interaction between these two distinct aspects of Irish cultural and historical self-awareness: the metropolitan and the subaltern.

References

1 Based on the keynote lecture at the Conference on '1798: Revolution, Memory, Imagination', held by the Committee for the Study of Anglo-Irish Literature, Royal Irish Academy, 27-28 March 1998. Most of the Irish historical and literary materials referred to here are presented in greater detail in my books *Mere Irish and Fíor-Ghael* and *Remembrance and Imagination* (both Cork University Press, 1996). I owe special thanks to Ann Rigney and to Rolf Loeber.

2 The historiography of the period has been well charted by Donal McCartney's article 'The Writing of History in Ireland, 1800-1830', *Irish Historical Studies*, 10, no. 40 (Sept 1957): 347-362. In fictional writing, initial post-1800 publications (scant on the whole, some 25 titles in all) are memoirs thinly narrativized or fictionalized, with a sudden and brief outburst of novelistic treatment in the 1820s; I base this impression on the magnificent database-in-progress by Rolf Loeber and Magda Loeber-Stouthamer, *Literary Fiction as a Mirror of the Times: A Guide to Irish Fiction Published in Europe and North America* (cf. rloe+@pitt.edu); the compilers kindly let me have the benefit of their magnum opus for this purpose.

3 For the 'sublime' nature of Carlyle's historiography, see Ann Rigney, 'The Untenanted Places of the Past: Thomas Carlyle and the Varieties of Historical Ignorance', *History and Theory* 22 (1996): 338-57.

1798 in 1898: The Politics of Commemoration

SENIA PASETA

Dissension and deep division characterised late nineteenth-century Irish nationalism. Constitutional nationalists had been at odds since the early 1890s when the fall of C.S. Parnell had provoked a split in the Irish Parliamentary Party, while the Irish Republican Brotherhood was being undermined by the recently-established Irish National Alliance. The commemoration of the centenary of 1798 presented a remarkable propaganda opportunity to Irish nationalists of every hue, and proved especially appealing to those strategists who entertained hopes of political *rapprochement*. The commemoration attracted both established nationalists whose political careers were in dire need of resuscitation, and young, advanced nationalists eager to make their mark on the Irish political scene.

Fin de siècle Ireland witnessed numerous commemorations which fostered lively political discourse and presented vital propaganda opportunities for politicians who had been starved of publicity in post-Parnellite Ireland. The '98 centenary celebrations were influenced by concurrent commemorations just as they subsequently influenced the opposition which grew up around controversies such as the Boer War and the royal visits of 1900 and 1903. Queen Victoria's Diamond Jubilee in 1897 started, in the words of Michael McCarthy, the beginning of 'a host of jubilees and centennial celebrations'. McCarthy pronounced himself 'certain' that the 'celebrators of these other affairs took no part in the diamond jubilee'.[1] It is significant that the '98 Centenary Committee first assembled on the evening of 4 March, Emmet's birthday and jubilee day.

Under the chairmanship of John O'Leary, the Provisional Centenary Committee announced its intention to preside over a non-political and non-sectarian campaign which would welcome representatives of various organisations. But the centenary preparations were dominated at first by a clique of advanced nationalists, some of whom stamped their radicalism on the movement from its inception. When members of the Centenary Committee allegedly refused to organise anti-Jubilee demonstrations, James Connolly and the Irish Socialist Republican Party took matters into their own hands, staging a demonstration which could be heard by members of the Provisional Centenary Committee as they met in the Town Hall. Some Centenary Committee delegates, including Maud Gonne and W.B. Yeats, left their own meeting to observe Connolly's protests and accompanied a coffin which represented the British Empire and which was later thrown into the Liffey. The evening ended in violence as Connolly was arrested and crowds attending an open-air lantern slide display demonstrating scenes of British oppression clashed with police.

The council of the Young Ireland League met in 1896 to consider the forthcoming centenary. Founded in 1891, this organisation included John O'Leary and Yeats who endowed it with a literary-Fenian feel. The form of the centenary celebrations had been discussed by advanced nationalists since the early 1890s, and by 1897 a wide network of IRB influenced centenary clubs had been established throughout Ireland and England. The movement assumed an international character from its inception and representatives from as far afield as America, France, South Africa and Australia became a feature of centenary events. Secretary of the IRB Supreme Council, Frederick Allen, became one of the movement's chief architects, hoping that the centenary would 'put a little national spirit into the young men here, and Lord knows they want it'. [2]

Unfortunately for Allen, the attempts by various nationalist alliances to control what 'national spirit' there was ensured that the '98 centenary was marred by factionalism almost from its inception. The Central Centenary Committee of Great Britain, for example, was beset by the competing claims for supremacy of several constitutional and republican nationalist blocs. Some of this arose because of the loyalty of many members to the Irish National Alliance, the militant organisation founded by dissident members of Clan na Gael in opposition to the IRB. Yeats was president of the British organisation, and like other members he became increasingly identified with the radical INA, thus alienating both IRB sympathisers and various IPP factions. Frank Hugh O'Donnell only made matters worse by publicly associating the Committee with a radical and anti-parliamentary party position and thereby antagonising other members including Yeats.[3]

O'Leary's Dublin group, meanwhile, was beset by its own set of disputes, many of them caused by the increasing involvement of parliamentarians in preparations for the centenary. The parliamentarians were of course themselves split into several factions and each camp endeavoured to play a role in the Centenary celebrations and to shift attention from advanced nationalists to themselves. John Dillon and John Redmond led the constitutional factions in their attempts to win positions on the Centenary Committee.[4] Capturing the 'national mood' was in itself important to them, but using the '98 Centenary to steer the divided party towards reunification became crucial. Constitutional nationalist attempts to install their own members on the Centennial Committee revealed the endurance of Parnellite allegiances. As leader of the small group of party men who had stayed loyal to Parnell, Redmond maintained some influence in Fenian circles, but he found that this did not ensure automatic association with the Centenary Committee. Non-sitting constitutionalists had been allowed positions on the Committee, but sitting MPs were resolutely kept out. Dillon fared no better and after making a series of attempts to align himself with the London Committee and Belfast nationalists, his own faction launched a rival organisation, the United Irishmen Centennial Association.

Dillon's astute political manoeuvring and eventual success in disrupting the Dublin committee and forcing an amalgamation between his own and O'Learys's group has been thoroughly documented elsewhere, and is perhaps best illustrated by the unlikely spectacle of Dillon, Redmond and O'Leary together laying the foundation stone for the proposed 1798 memorial in April, 1898.[5] Despite the enthusiastic republicanism expressed by so many of the early organisers of the Centenary celebrations, it is clear that once constitutional nationalists flexed their political muscle and influence, they could not be prevented from all but dominating '98 events. Dillon's ability to stamp constitutional nationalism on the year's events displayed his political prowess; the way in which he convinced the Dublin committee to agree to allow party members to join its executive anticipated the Irish Party's subsequent policy of colonising nationalist organisations which threatened to shift attention away from the Party.

If commemorating the 1798 rebellion posed interpretative difficulties for the constitutionalists, they kept it well hidden, presenting instead a whole-hearted endorsement of the '98 rebels in ways which committed them to the constitutional path to Home Rule. Redmond latched on to those '98 ideals which best suited the interests of a unified and influential Irish Party by acknowledging that the 1798 rebellion had been a military disaster, but emphasising that:

> Irishmen of all shades of Nationalist opinion, divided as they are into many sections upon the politics of that day, are uniting as one man to celebrate its centenary.[6]

The '98 centenary also invited the construction of historical surveys and Redmond and his *Freeman's Journal* grasped the opportunity to present the reading public with the history of Ireland as seen through constitutional eyes. Redmond's most ambitious article presented the story of the legacy of the Union of Ireland and Great Britain which inevitably highlighted famine, repression, and economic degradation. He added, however, that Ireland was:

> making its way politically, at least – slowly but surely. The blood of the martyrs of '98 was not shed in vain. The efforts and sacrifices of the men of '48, '65 and '67 have borne fruit. The statesmanship of Parnell not only achieved much, but will yet inspire the whole Irish nation to brave and wise deeds for its liberation.[7]

Redmond's message left little to the imagination: the republicanism espoused by 1798 rebels and their nineteenth-century fellow travellers should be viewed as but one episode in Ireland's historical progression towards sovereignty, a course of which Redmond, as Parnell's successor, was now in charge. Maud Gonne might well have despaired of the constitutionalists who 'eulogis[ed] Wolf Tone and tr[ied] to keep the people from following his teaching',[8] but Redmond continued to feed those same 'people' his constitutional and whiggish interpretation of Irish History. The United Irishmen, he assured his readers, had been established to secure Catholic emancipation and 'parliamentary reform'. He could hardly avoid admitting that Wolf Tone was himself a separatist revolutionary, but the United Irishmen – 'an open and constitutional organisation' – only took up arms when the implementation of peaceful reform seemed impossible.[9] English coercion and failure to sanction reform was thus to blame for the transformation of an essentially parliamentary movement into a revolutionary one. In a piece intended to send warning messages to English statesmen and to his estranged fellow constitutionalists, Redmond claimed that the failure to endorse his programme might have dire consequences:

> Its [the '98 centenary] intensity will be increased by the temporary breakdown of Parliamentary and Constitutional methods which have followed from the abandonment and destruction of Mr Parnell, and it will be an evidence that, if only the means were at hand, Irishmen would not be loathe again to take up the weapons of revolution to forward their ends. This much the demonstration will certainly mean, and if it succeeds in destroying the idea that because Ireland to-day is peaceful and crimeless therefore she has abandoned the national struggle it will have served a useful end.[10]

When required, Redmond could wrap himself in a revolutionary cloak by virtue of his support for Parnell and his good relations with many Fenians, thus linking himself with Ireland's radical past. But Ireland in 1898 rather than Ireland in 1798 became the focus of his campaigning throughout the centenary year. He asserted, for example, that 'there is no reason for despair', offering the imminent implementation of 'a wide measure of local self-government' as one of the reasons for his optimism. William O'Brien, leader of the newly-established and significantly named United Irish League, similarly pounced on the issue of local government, announcing, for example, during a speech given at a centenary event: 'the whole local government of the country, with all its powers and revenues, will be our own'.[11]

Dillon believed that the enthusiasm created by the centennial celebrations could be conducive to the reunion of the Irish Party and that the United Irish League must play a significant role in the unification process.[12] He hoped that nationalists who had been 'unhappily separated from each other for the past eight years would in the great centenary celebrations find a common platform, would stand together . . .'[13]

Given the monumental rise of the United Irish League and the revival of advanced nationalism afforded by the centenary celebrations, the warring IPP factions could hardly afford to maintain their enmity any longer, and the leading lights of the main factions began to appear together on '98 platforms. Indeed Dillon and Redmond played major roles at the year's crowning event, the laying of a foundation stone for the Wolfe Tone memorial on 15 August.[14] It is not surprising that Maud Gonne felt 'depressed' during the ceremony for it signified the strength of the constitutionalist campaign.[15] The people who assembled to watch the August ceremony were confronted with representatives of Irish nationalism, old and new. Although John O'Leary presided over the event, it was clear that the influence of old-style Fenianism was on the decline and moreover, that it had lacked the vigour to withstand the onslaught of the parliamentarians. Advanced nationalist attempts to raise money for the 1798 memorial paralleled the decline of the IRB old guard: only £561 of the estimated £14,000 needed to erect the monument was raised,[16] and it was 1967 before the memorial itself was actually unveiled.

How then does one assess Arthur Griffith's claim that 1898 was 'the beginning of all modern efforts towards a return to the ideals of independence'?[17] An interesting place to begin is with the ceremony itself for it was there that William Rooney delivered a stirring speech in Irish and Yeats proclaimed:

> This immense demonstration is being held at a momentous time in Irish history. England has persuaded herself that Ireland, discredited by dissension, was about to submit. England had persuaded herself that she could settle the Irish question by a handful of arms. We have answered England by this great demonstration. She is no longer deceived. She now knows that Ireland cherishes the same spirit still.[18]

This neo-Fenian affirmation of the Irish 'spirit' would have been familiar to Irish nationalists, but neither Yeats, Gonne nor Rooney subscribed fully to the orthodox Fenian faith. Rather, they represented the new nationalism which was subsequently harnessed by Arthur Griffith who was himself deeply influenced by Rooney. Unlike the IRB, this new nationalism boasted youth, openness and journalistic genius. Confrontational, flamboyant and usually contemptuous of the official IPP policy which the majority of nationalist Ireland subscribed to, Griffith's nationalism was comprised of strands of Fenian and Young Ireland dogma, but it also owed much to the literary and debating clubs which had emerged in the 1880s and 1890s. Many of these early societies were deeply influenced by the Parnell split, but they had begun to emerge before Parnell's death and during the 1890s became less interested in conventional politics, turning instead to literary matters which they often viewed through a political lens.

Founded in 1893, the Celtic Literary Society succeeded the Leinster Literary Society, its change of name indicative of the shift in focus of its growing membership. Griffith joined the society in 1895 and although he left for South Africa the following year, many of the topics discussed at the society's meetings reflected his subsequent preoccupations.[19] The political and expressive significance of the 1798 rebellion appealed to many supporters of these small societies for whom the '98 rebels occupied a natural place in Ireland's glorious past, and it is not surprising that many of the early groups established to discuss the centenary year were themselves literary and debating associations. Sympathetic as many of them were to a particular version of Irish history which emphasised the villainy of the Saxon, they could hardly fail to be inspired by the heroism, betrayal and martyrdom associated with the 1798 rebellion.

Although influential supporters like Yeats eventually parted company with Griffith, lively new provocateurs such as Edward Martyn, John MacBride and Arthur Lynch supported Griffith's early political campaigns. First and foremost was the nationalist opposition to the Boer War which many constitutional and physical-force nationalists subscribed to, but which came increasingly under the influence of Griffith and his *United Irishman*. Meetings of the newly-established Irish Transvaal Committee took place in the rooms of the Celtic Literary Society and activists included Yeats, Griffith and Gonne. Griffith's widening network of supporters subsequently led the spectacular protests against the royal visits of Queen Victoria in 1900 and King Edward VII in 1903.

Antipathy towards the Irish Party became more pronounced. Griffith described the reunification of the Party in 1900 as 'sordid', and led the campaign to discredit it over its position on the Boer War. The propaganda produced by his Irish Transvaal Committee advised Irish men to 'Remember '98' before enlisting in the British army. His condemnation of what he described as the IPP's policy of 'Home Rule plus the Empire' was not unlike the kind of anti-IPP rhetoric he subsequently produced in response to the Party's support for the British War effort between 1914 and 1918.

It is clear that the 1898 commemorations were motivated as much by contemporary political concerns as they were by the desire to memorialise the 1798 Uprising. The 1890s had witnessed the fragmentation of the precarious nationalist alliances which had been held together by Parnell, and his fall from power in 1891 ushered in a lack-lustre period for Irish nationalism. The Griffith-led protests occupied a useful middle ground between the nationalism espoused by the IPP and the old physical force tradition rejected by Griffith. They could not be described as popular and certainly did not constitute a united front, but they appealed to radicals on the margins of nationalist activity, most of whom were involved with and influenced by Irish cultural revivalism. These men and women spearheaded the 'new nationalism' which subsequently developed through organisations including Cumann na nGaedheal, the Dungannon Clubs and Inghinidhe na hÉireann. They had been radicalised and had themselves radicalised Irish politics in the crucial period, 1897–1903. Their opposition to imperialism, conventional nationalism and English cultural influences became crucial components of the emerging Sinn Féin and of a new era in Irish nationalist politics.

Notes and References

1 Other events included the fiftieth anniversary of the death of Daniel O'Connell and various ecclesiastical commemorations: M. McCarthy, *Five Years in Ireland, 1895–1900* (Dublin and London, 1903), p. 260

2 F.J. Allen to John Devoy, 29 December, 1897; cited in T.J. O'Keefe, 'The 1898 Efforts to Celebrate the United Irishmen: The '98 Centennial', *Éire-Ireland*, vol. xxiii, 1988, pp. 54-5.

3 R.F. Foster, *W.B. Yeats, A Life: The Apprentice Mage* (Oxford University Press, 1997), pp. 189-91.

4 O'Keefe, 'The 1898 Efforts to Celebrate the United Irishmen', pp. 56-7.

5 See ibid. for an excellent analysis of the political machinations which occurred behind the scenes.

6 J.E. Redmond, 'The Centenary of '98', *Nineteenth Century*, vol. xliii, 1898, p. 612.

7 J.E. Redmond, 'Ireland Since '98', *North American Review*, vol. clxvi, 1898, p. 397.

8 M. Gonne, *A Servant of the Queen*, 2nd edn (Dublin: Golden Eagle, 1950), p. 273.

9 Redmond, 'The Centenary of '98', p. 616.

10 Ibid, p. 612.

11 *Freeman's Journal*, 3 October, 1898. I am indebted to Angela Murphy for this reference.

12 F.S.L. Lyons, *John Dillon: A Biography* (London: Routledge and Kegan Paul, 1968), p. 191.

13 *Freeman's Journal*, 10 October, 1898.

14 Ibid, 16 August, 1898.

15 Gonne, *A Servant of the Queen*, p. 274.

16 L. Ó Broin, *Revolutionary Underground: The Story of the Irish Republican Brotherhood, 1858–1924* (Dublin: Gill and Macmillan, 1976), p. 91 and Foster, *W.B. Yeats*, p. 191.

17 Griffith quoted in M. Bourke, *John O'Leary: A Study in Irish Separatism* (Tralee, 1967), p. 216.

18 Yeats quoted in M.F. Ryan, *Fenian Memories* (Dublin: M.H. Gill, 1945), p. 188.

19 See R. Davis, *Arthur Griffith and Non-Violent Sinn Féin* (Dublin: Anvil, 1974), pp. 3-16 for a discussion of Griffith's early influences and development.

20 *Freeman's Journal*, 6 January, 1900.

REVIEW ARTICLE*

1798 and the United Irishmen

TOM DUNNE

The first major reassessment of 1798 since Lecky, Thomas Pakenham's *The Year of Liberty* (1969), opened with three, brief statements that set the tone for what followed, a racy account, strong on the human mess and suffering of the rebellion, and lacking the usual nationalist pieties.

> The rebellion of 1798 is the most violent and tragic event in Irish history between the Jacobite wars and the Great Famine.
>
> In the space of a few weeks, 30,000 people – peasants armed with pikes and pitchforks, defenceless women and children – were cut down or shot or blown like chaff as they charged up to the mouth of the cannon.
>
> The result of the rebellion was no less disastrous: Britain imposed a Union on terms that proved unacceptable to the majority of the Irish people, and there was a legacy of violence and hatred that has persisted to the present day.

*The books reviewed here are: Nancy J. Curtin. *The United Irishmen. Popular politics in Ulster and Dublin, 1791–1798.* Clarendon Press, Oxford, 1994, ISBN 0-19-820322-5; A.T.Q. Stewart. *The Summer Soldiers. The 1798 rebellion in Antrim and Down.* The Blackstaff Press, Belfast, 1995, ISBN 0-85640-558-2; Kevin Whelan. *The Tree of Liberty. Radicalism, Catholicism and the construction in Irish identity 1760–1830.* Cork University Press, 1996, ISBN 1-85918-060-4; D. Keogh and N. Furlong (eds). *The Mighty Wave. The 1798 rebellion in Wexford.* Four Courts Press, Dublin, 1996, ISBN 185182-254-2; Daniel Gahan. *The People's Rising: Wexford, 1798.* Gill and Macmillan, Dublin, 1995, ISBN 07171 23235; Thomas Pakenham. *The Year of Liberty. The great Irish rebellion of 1798.* Weidenfeld and Nicolson, London (revised edition), 1997, ISBN 0 297 819550; Charles Dickson. *The Wexford Rising in 1798.* Constable, London (1997 ed.), ISBN 0 09 4772509; S.W. Myers and D.E. McKnight (eds). *Memoirs of the different rebellions in Ireland from the arrival of the English: also, a particular detail of that which broke out the 23rd May 1798, with the history of the conspiracy which preceded it.* by Sir Richard Musgrave. Round Tower Books, Indiana and Duffy Press, Enniscorthy (4th edition, 1995), ISBN 0-9643925-0-X; D. Keogh and N. Furlong (eds). *The Women of 1798.* Four Courts Press, Dublin, 1998, ISBN 1-85182-359-X.

Pakenham's book remains controversial. Colm Tóibín recalls an expression of anger at a launch in Wexford and admits that he can still find 'the tone and the use of the language offensive and hurtful'.[1] This feeling is shared by Daniel Gahan, who remembers his upset at its image of the rebels, and even now sees it as ('unwittingly perhaps') a revival of the old loyalist view, best exemplified by Musgrave, in which 'the rebels were an unruly mob, cowardly but cruel, and motivated above all by religious hatred'. Pakenham himself had pointed out that while 'sources are embarrassingly rich on the loyalist side', he had found fewer than a hundred on the rebel side, and being thus forced to rely on second-hand and second-rate reports, such as from informers and ballads, it was 'impossible to avoid giving offence'.

In the intervening thirty years our understanding of the background to the rebellion has been transformed, particularly by the work of Tom Powell, Louis Cullen, Kevin Whelan and Daniel Gahan on Wexford's complex economic, social and cultural crisis during the 1790s. Yet the new narrative histories under review, while they have more detail and a somewhat more sympathetic tone, do not change Pakenham's account or analysis significantly. This reflects an enduring problem of inadequate sources, particularly for the motivation of the rebels in the south east. No significant new sources have come to light, and, with one important exception, there has been relatively little radical reinterpretation of those available to Pakenham. The exception is Cullen's influential challenge to the long accepted view (first articulated by the United Irishmen themselves) that there was no significant United Irish organisation in Wexford prior to the rebellion. His main sources are a list, possibly of United Irish 'captains', first published by Musgrave (1801), and scattered references to military ranks of rebel leaders. Using his unrivalled knowledge of local and family history, particularly of kinship networks and their role in radical politics, he projected a United Irish organisation that made new sense, particularly of the outbreak and early course of the rebellion. This brilliant hypothesis has informed much of the new research, particularly by Kevin Whelan; at the same time, however, it has been reduced to the crude slogan 'The United Irish Revolution', in the literature of 'Comóradh '98', the body established by Wexford County Council to organise the bicentenary. It is now also the official government view, a politically correct version of 1798, giving a historical dimension to the 'peace process' which, to quote the Taoiseach, Bertie Ahern, will 'fulfil some of the ideals of the United Irishmen'. I have dealt elsewhere with the politicisation of the bicentenary and its wilder fantasies of a 'Wexford Republic' and 'Senate'.[2] It forms an important context, however, for understanding aspects of the new historiography which, like the old, reflects changing political perspectives and concerns.

One hope of this new emphasis is to connect the outbreak in Wexford and surrounding counties with that in Antrim and Down, traditionally seen as United Irish not only in organisation, but in its almost chivalric, idealistic character. Some of the ways in which the United Irish movement changed in its turbulent short lifetime have been traced in important recent work, particularly by Marianne Elliott, but only with Nancy Curtin's landmark study, *The United Irishmen: popular politics in Ulster and Dublin 1791–98*, do we get a comprehensive analysis of its shifting engagement with local issues and popular culture. She too points to limited sources, so that the picture 'must be filtered through the lens of magistrates, office holders and informers'. Her ability to use such sources imaginatively and sympathetically and to combine them with the patchy, often difficult internal evidence, is one of the great strengths of this exceptional book. Stressing the United Irish 'genius for propaganda' she is particularly good on how this 'represented the union of republican theory and republican practice', and how it tried, above all, 'to make every man a citizen', in accordance with its initial and enduring core value of civic humanism. At the heart of her analysis, and of United Irish difficulties, was the attempted alliance between these 'petty bourgeois revolutionaries', 'deeply immersed in British radical Whig culture' and the dynamic but essentially sectarian Catholic secret society, the Defenders, who 'sought a reversal of the conquest'. That alliance, together with the paralysis induced by the focus on French intervention, ultimately contributed to a once formidable organisation becoming not only ineffectual but compromised. The tension inherent in trying to organise 'a mass-based conspiracy', particularly when the focus was as much on propaganda as on revolutionary organisation, is particularly well drawn. The most original contributions of this detailed, nuanced study are in chapters on organisation, recruitment and social composition, and propaganda (both literary and 'propaganda by deed'). United Irish successes were spectacular: 'never again did an underground republican movement enjoy as massive a following or as formidable or extensive an organisation as the United Irishmen'. This strength was draining away, however, even before the rebellion, under the pressures of state repression, economic expansion and sectarian polarisation, and in the end, sectarianism proved more powerful than republican virtue. Sadly, the United Irishmen themselves contributed substantially to this sectarian surge as Cullen and Whelan demonstrated years ago in the case of Wexford. Curtin concludes 'that the United Irishmen themselves were largely responsible, through their emotional propaganda for turning peasant fears into vengeful paranoia, for exacerbating sectarian tensions'.

Curtin's final chapter focuses her detailed knowledge of the United Irish organisation and its links to popular culture and politics on the rebellion in Ulster, where, as one contemporary put it, 'the spirit of rebellion took its birth', and 'where lies the hopes, the spring, the wealth and the force of the United Irishmen'. And there, despite the dampening effects of government repression, and the successful depiction ('sadly well founded to some extent') of the already rampant outbreak in Wexford as 'a popish rebellion', the turnout was significant: 'the numbers were there; it was leadership and opportunity were wanting'. But the initial numbers also flattered to deceive, not least because of the defection of Defender contingents at key moments, and the disillusionment of many Presbyterians with the core proposition of 'United Irishmen'. One Antrim leader was reported as declaring, on the steps of the scaffold: 'he knew well that had the *north* been successful, *they* would have had to fight the battle over again with the Catholics of the south'.

Glimpses of this critical fault line can be got from A.T.Q. Stewart's engaging narrative history, *The Summer Soldiers: the 1798 rebellion in Antrim and Down*. Almost uniquely among Irish historians, Stewart combines historical scholarship of the highest order with a polished literary style. A major historian of the early United Irishmen, he shares many of their perspectives and sympathies. He wears his great learning lightly, offering little enough by way of formal analysis and allowing the participants on all sides (often brought alive in vivid rapid sketches) to speak for themselves. He is particularly good on the continuity of the old Volunteering culture (including uniforms and weapons) into the rebellion, and the complex contribution of radical (and not so radical) Presbyterianism, including the 'kind of Sabbath sobriety' that marked the rebel camp before the crucial and bloody engagement of Ballinahinch. The story features heroic deeds, but even more, repeated rapid collapse and confusion, even after initial success. Compared to Wexford, it seemed an altogether more tentative affair, with comparatively few casualties or sectarian outrages. Clearly, more can be said than either Curtin or Stewart manage on the Presbyterian/Episcopalian dimensions of the Ulster rebellion, particularly at local level. Likewise the role of the Defenders needs to be understood better. Their conflict with the United Irishmen appears here in rare incidents, as in the symbolic differences between the green flags carried by republicans at Randelstown and those of the Defenders who added a cross, and on one banner the slogan, 'Remember Armagh' (i.e. the anti-Catholic atrocities of some years earlier).

Curtin's analysis by occupation of the 'activist core' of 1,732 United Irishmen found that the agricultural sector accounted for only 13 per cent compared with 76 per cent from commercial, and professional sectors. This may help to account for the comparatively poor state of the organisation in Wexford (even if Cullen's hypothesis was fully endorsed, it involves a late and patchy development, however influential). This prosperous, relatively peaceful county was indeed predominantly agricultural, but it was also, as Louis Cullen has shown, 'a more complex county than meets the eye'. His analysis stresses the conflict among gentry/middlemen families particularly in the north of the county, where they were strongly and uniquely divided on sectarian lines and were subject to intensifying economic pressures prior to the rebellion. Ultimately the younger generation of radicalised Catholic middlemen spearheaded the late United Irish recruitment drive (partly exploiting sectarian fears) and the core conflict in 1798 was between them and the ultra-loyalist, increasingly Orange yeomanry, led by their Protestant rivals. Cullen's analysis, made in a series of key contributions during the 1980s,[3] was further developed by fellow-Wexfordman Kevin Whelan. His layered mapping of an often bewildering array of factors brought exciting new perspectives then emerging in historical geography to wider notice, and rapidly made him the most distinctive, and, to my mind, the most important of a talented new generation of historians. Much of his early work focused on Catholicism, its regional differentiation and its relationship to modernisation and, increasingly, to politics. His main contributions until recently on the 1798 rebellion in Wexford have been on 'the role of the Catholic priests', and on 'the religious factor'. The latter, in a 1987 paper, was partly traced in a still indispensable series of maps, for example of Protestants killed and Catholic chapels burned – both clustered heavily in the northern part of the county. As well as further stressing the sectarian basis of gentry rivalry, he dealt with 'the still tenuous figure of the Defender' and 'the equally vague figure of the Orangemen', both late arrivals on the scene, but exploited by the equally new United Irishmen. Looking particularly at the targeting of relatively recent Protestant newcomers like the Palatines, he found, in 1987, 'a purely sectarian motive . . . evident in many of the killings' by the rebels.[4]

Whelan's important collection of essays (all but one published previously, though this is not acknowledged), *The Tree of Liberty*, is offered specifically as a contribution to the bicentenary of 1798. However, its much wider scope is indicated in its subtitle, 'Radicalism, Catholicism and the construction of Irish identity 1760–1830', although, surprisingly, it does not deal directly with the rebellion itself. The focus is cultural/political; there are no maps, but in even fuller spate than before is that other Whelan characteristic – the tumbling flood of colourful, often electrifying, sometimes mystifying language and the pell-mell of ideas chasing one another like the boulders of ice cascading over Niagra (yes it's catching!). There is also a clear present-day agenda, expressed with disarming frankness in the preface. His aim is to make the 1790s 'available in a fresh way, opening a generous space which has been artificially constricted'. The 'enduring relevance' of the 1790s is 'the window of opportunity which opened up and was forcibly closed', and which involved the idea of 'a non-sectarian, democratic and inclusive politics'. He declares, 'the project remains uncompleted; understanding the reason for its momentous defeat in the 1790s can help in ensuring that history does not repeat itself in the 1990s'. The preface also tells us that 'the informing perspective in these essays is post-revisionist', which modish stance is defined in part as involving 'a self-conscious heave beyond the comforting polarities of "nationalist" and "revisionist" history'. A key question about this important and already influential book must be how successful or sustained this 'heave' is, and in particular whether 'post-revisionist' here, as in the case of some recent famine studies which defined themselves in the same way, isn't a rehabilitated rather than a transcended nationalist perspective, a new version of the 'essentialism' it is determined to avoid.

These essays are constantly aware of the battleground of historiography, and might best be approached by taking the final (and only entirely new) essay first. Entitled ''98 after 98: the politics of memory' this is a *tour-de-force*, a learned, often dazzling, always passionate analysis of the politics of the accounts and interpretations of 1798; 'the rebellion never passed into history because it never passed out of politics'. This is as true of his own work, as of any of those he excoriates, yet the tone is not only of impatience, it tends cumulatively to omniscience. The core of his analysis is expressed in his blunt dismissal of Pakenham's *Year of Liberty* as 'fundamentally wrong', above all because 'he emphasises sectarianism and depoliticises the rebels'. In this he is shown to be in a long tradition; despite very different political perspectives and agendas, this is also the basic emphasis of the Ultra-Protestant, Musgrave; of early Catholic accounts, like Hay's; of liberal Protestant accounts, like Gordon's, of local United Irish participants, like Cloney and national leaders like Emmet and McNevan; and of the biggest single influence on modern perspectives, Fr Kavanagh's 'Faith and Fatherland' account 'of heroic priest-leaders and of goaded but morally pure, peasantry'. Battling valiantly against this flood, fed by so many tributaries, are the marginalised voices, 'reclaiming the rebellion', particularly those of R.R. Madden, Luke Cullen and Miles Byrne (and now Whelan). The *Memoirs* of Byrne, published in 1863, after a distinguished career in the French army, and 'in detached old age' seem to offer the viewpoint with which Whelan most identifies, and which he summarises as: 'the rebellion was not a disjointed response to unbearable provocation, but one coherently organised by a secret society with mass popular support'. This analysis of the historiography and its underlying politics is illuminating, but also distorting. Like the sweep of a searchlight beam its objective is simply to expose malefactors and it admits no shadows. For example, in Musgrave, as in Madden and Luke Cullen, partisan explanation is balanced (indeed overwhelmed) by a mass of raw primary material, which can often point to very different conclusions. And even Byrne's account is far from any simple vindication of the notion of a United Irish rebellion. His description of the spread of 'the united irish system' prior to the rebellion sits oddly with his account of the campaign as a spontaneous response to persecution, led by priests, especially John Murphy, the hero of his account, and nowhere in it linked to the United Irishmen. His assertion that 'nothing could be further from their views than a religious war' is genuine, but he portrays the rebellion much more as a matter of self-defence against a 'war of extermination' by 'cruel Orangemen', rather than (as he also described it) a war 'to set Ireland independent and free'. His dominant emphasis is 'that the Irish people were not making a religious struggle but were carrying on a just war of self-defence against the most unheard of tyranny'.[5]

As in Byrne, Whelan's repeated denial of a sectarian dimension to 1798 can be read as betraying unease about the overwhelming evidence for a contrary reality, and which he knows better than anyone. His essay on that topic in *The Tree of Liberty* is subtitled, 'the state and sectarianism in the 1790s', and its argument is that state-sponsored sectarianism was part of 'counter-revolutionary strategy'. There was, apparently, no Catholic sectarianism (until Whelan's *bêté noire*, O'Connell, that is) and the only relationship of the United Irishmen to the phenomenon was in a failure to understand 'how these atavistic feelings could have any genuine popular constituency'. He points to their attempts 'to smooth sectarian tensions in Armagh', but has not a word about their activities in Wexford, 'in exploiting and exacerbating sectarian tension', such as those he noted ten years earlier. His call for more attention to be paid to the importance of 'popular loyalism' is important, but it is immensely disappointing that his one-sided analysis of pre-rebellion sectarianism can only lead to the grudging, indeed almost coded, conclusion that because they 'misjudged the depth of popular anti-revolutionary sentiment . . . the United Irish revolution turned out not to be a painless coup, but a rancorous struggle, in which the lines of demarcation all too easily split along confessional cleavages' – in other words, the rebellion turned into a bitterly sectarian conflict!

Still moving backwards through this fascinating book, the previous essay, 'The republic in the village: the United Irishmen, the Enlightenment and popular culture' covers much of the same ground as Curtin, and further illuminates the intensity and complexity of the politicisation drive, targeted at tenants and artisans, and is particularly interesting on the appeal to Dublin's 'political underground'. The idea that the United Irishmen used existing social and cultural formations like faction groups, hurling teams, mayboys and parishes offers one direct link between 'the Enlightenment' and 'popular culture', but while there is evidence that such traditional forms of identity were used as a *modus vivendi* during the rebellion, not even Byrne links this specifically to the development of a cell system by the United Irishmen. Lacking here is not only Curtin's perspective on United Irish politicisation involving some exploitation of sectarian tensions, but also any testing of it against what evidence we have for the *mentalité*, of the rebels, for example in the highly sectarian ballads collected by Madden, among others. This is where Whelan's failure to emulate Curtin and test his analysis against the evidence of the rebellion itself most weakens his argument. Even if 'the republic' did become part of 'the village' in the years prior to the outbreak, he hardly believes that it entirely replaced more traditional (but equally 'political') perspectives? We have much to learn about popular culture from the Defenders, hardly mentioned here, although a much less 'tenuous' phenomenon after the work of Smyth and others, than they were ten years ago. Gaelic sources may be even more important. Whelan's confident assertion that 'the rebellion of 1798 was an episode in English-speaking, not Irish-speaking Ireland' ignores significant evidence, particularly for the key barony of Bantry, and reflects an over-reliance on the evidence of the more anglicised middlemen/gentry figures, who are the key to the little we ever can understand of the United Irish organisation in Wexford. The clear focus on the group makes his first essay, 'An underground gentry? Catholic Middlemen in eighteenth-century Ireland', the best in the collection, and it's a pity that its insights into the Jacobite tradition were not applied to the democratisation of that tradition from the 1780s. The focus is still on *mentalité*, especially as it 'refocused from residually Jacobite to incipiently Jacobin forms' but this essay also illuminates major areas of social and cultural development, such as the rise of the Catholic big farmer class and its relationship to the middlemen/gentry world, not least as inheritors of the claim to be the true owners of forfeited estates. The pervasiveness of this view, and the extent of Ascendancy obsession with it, is brought to light in a wholly new way. This is Whelan at his best, a bold and imaginative thesis, supported by unrivalled knowledge of the manuscript sources and the ability to produce dozens of local examples, from all corners of the country. The ability to illuminate the argument by the introduction of a whole new dimension of evidence is unrivalled. Thus, arguing that the Catholic middlemen of the eighteenth century combined effective gentry status, with strong links to popular culture, he says of one such family's home:

> The Sweetman House at Newbawn is a visual representation of this polyvalent world expressed in architectural terms. The house which they built there in the 1690s still survives – a fine two-storeyed, five-bayed structure of imposing dimensions. It is an instructive example of the blend of the traditional and formal in architectural styles: the traditional elements encompass the thatched roof, the mud and coarse rubble walls, the iron window-bars and the central chimney; the formal elements include the symmetrical facade, the Gibbsian doorcase and the sashed windows. The house embodied exactly the social position of the Sweetman family, partaking of both the gentry and common traditions.

It is a great pity that a similar awareness of the blend of traditional and modern in the politicisation of the Wexford rural community in the 1790s is so lacking in the later chapters, where the tradition of Catholic sectarian politics is utterly discounted. This is a collection of essays at odds with itself and with much of the earlier work of this exceptional historian. It is to be hoped that, when the fever of this bicentenary year abates, and when 1798 becomes a little less entangled with contemporary politics, Kevin Whelan will carry through this complex analysis of his 'underground gentry' into the yet more tangled and elusive question of politicisation in the 1790s.

Whelan's is the lead paper in the conference volume, *The Mighty Wave: the 1798 Rebellion in Wexford*, edited by Dáire Keogh and Nicholas Furlong. It reiterates the main arguments of *The Tree of Liberty*, and is again particularly concerned to deny any significant sectarian dimension of the rebellion. In two respects it pushes the argument further. The present-day political agenda is articulated more forcibly. Anxious 'to ensure that history does not tragically repeat itself in the 1990s', he believes 'we must also relinquish our obsession . . . with pikes and deaths, murder, mayhem and martyrdom. We should instead stress the living principles of democracy and pluralism which the United Irishmen formulated'. Then, venturing into some analysis of the outbreak itself, he endorses fully one of the key contentions of 'Comóradh '98', claiming, 'Not just militarily but politically the United Irishmen in Wexford achieved a striking success in the short lived Wexford Republic which administered the county during the rebel occupation'. This is a startling claim for someone of Whelan's eminence to make, but it is supported only by reference to his own article of nearly ten years earlier in the volume on *Ireland and the French Revolution*, edited by Gough and Dickson.[6] This has a paragraph on the '"embryo republic" in Wexford town', which is here reproduced almost verbatim (except that the 'embryo' has now emerged fully formed and holds sway over the county as well as the town). The only reference given for this 'embryo republic' in the earlier paper is to Hay, who gives an interesting account of the 'committee' which tried to keep order and regulate the food supply during the rebel occupation of Wexford town, but nowhere mentions a 'Republic'. Nor does he mention a 'Senate', that other phantom of 'Comóradh '98' which Whelan also unproblematically declares a fact in his paper in *The Mighty Wave*. No documentary evidence is cited, for the very good reason that none exists.

Louis Cullen also revisits his earlier work in *The Mighty Wave* in an important paper, 'The United Irishmen in Wexford', which makes the case for significant United Irish direction of the rebellion in a more circumspect and persuasive way than Whelan. His conclusion that, 'it is hard to fall back on sectarianism as a general explanation', for example, doesn't exclude it from consideration. He also acknowledges the poor evidential base, even for key figures like Cloney and Kelly. Miles Byrne's *Memoirs* are also an important source for Cullen, and are examined by Thomas Bartlett in one of the best contributions to *The Mighty Wave*. He is particularly good on how the memoirs were shaped by Byrne's immersion in French military culture, which included a strong 'distaste for insurgency', and so Byrne 'constantly stressed the military discipline and good order maintained by the Irish rebels, in effect denying that they were insurgents'. An important related contribution is Daniel Gahan's on 'The military planning of the 1798 rebellion in Wexford', which follows Cullen's line on United Irish direction, but also reflects the problems with sources for this, and ends with the tentative conclusion that 'the strategic options that the rebels chose and the battle tactics they adopted are consistent with a movement inspired not by those on the margins of this society but by those at its centre'.

Thomas Bartlett believes that 'all previous accounts of the rebellion in Wexford are now superseded by Daniel Gahan's *The People's Rising*. It is certainly a lively, well-rounded narrative, which makes the most of often patchy sources, and when it embroiders on them, as perforce it often must, does so for the most part with skill and discernment. It is clear about 'the fragments of evidences we have' on the United Irish contribution, and dismissive of the claims made for a 'Republic of Wexford'. Its narrative drive (like that of virtually all accounts of the outbreak, whether in the earlier histories or contemporary ballads) is overdetermined by fitting it to the neat grid of a military campaign, and this allows little room for analysis, for example, of the agrarian dimensions, on which Gahan is a noted expert. Nor does Gahan avert the gaze from rebel atrocities, and focus only on those perpetrated by the army. However his concern to find an exact parallel for the most infamous rebel atrocity, that of Scullabogue, leads to the most startling finding of the book, and one that has already achieved wide currency. He claims that the shooting and burning to death of up to one hundred and fifty noncombatants (including women and children and virtually all Protestants) was probably preceded by 'the worst atrocity to be committed in the war so far', the deliberate burning to death of seventy wounded rebels in a 'makeshift hospital' in nearby New Ross, during the bloody battle that raged there that same morning. He has no new sources for the hitherto unnoticed atrocity, only a reinterpretation of the much-used accounts by Alexander and Cloney. I have pointed out elsewhere that these sources simply don't support Gahan's interpretation,[7] and I draw attention to it again, only as an example of how a particular 'revisionist' account can rapidly gain the status of undeniable fact when it resonates in a sympathetic political climate. 'Comóradh '98' has recently announced the erection of a plaque to commemorate this atrocity on the walls of a 'hospital' for which we have no evidence, nor indeed have we any means of identifying the building! This will complement the 'Comóradh '98' memorial on the site of Scullabogue, which is concerned only to deny any sectarian dimension to that atrocity and to record the regret of the United Irishmen. There can be few more extreme examples of 'commemoration' distorting the historical record in the interests of a contemporary political agenda. It's a pity that the manner in which Gahan's 'discovery' has been politicised makes it necessary to harp again on this aspect of a book which remains a substantial achievement, a sustained attempt at a balanced narrative from a sophisticated nationalist perspective.

Gahan's 'preface' attacks Thomas Pakenham's *The Year of Liberty* (1969) as 'a reborn version of the old loyalist interpretation . . . best exemplified by the work of Sir Richard Musgrave'. Pakenham and Musgrave (with Dickson's *The Wexford Rising*) are the most important of the reissues of this bicentenary year, and prove of more than merely curiosity or historiographical value. Although, admittedly, written before Irish historians had learned much about the complexity of popular culture or the politicisation of the poor, Pakenham is still remarkable for its focus on the sense of chaos and carnival that characterised phases of the rebellion; 'a people hardly marching – on the hike', as Seamus Heany described the rebels that same year. Pakenham's challenge that we confront 1798 as a 'most violent and tragic event' has been met in part by Gahan, but rejected by Whelan and almost entirely ignored by 'Comóradh '98'. Perhaps the oddest aspect of his account also features Scullabogue, which he chooses to describe *before* turning to the battle of New Ross. While this tends to load the narrative against the rebels, it can also be regarded as an extreme dramaticisation of what is true of all accounts of the rebellion, that, consciously or not, every reading of it is by the light of the lurid flames from Scullabogue barn. The lack of major new sources, and of convincing new interpretations leave Pakenham's account surprisingly intact, and it remains the only modern one that covers the outbreaks in Down, Antrim and Connaught, as well as the Leinster rebellion. However, it's a pity that in reissuing it, the opportunity was not taken to add a new preface, and not just a chronology and a glossary of terms. No one is better qualified to put the recent research and commemoration in context.

The reissue of Charles Dickson's *The Wexford Rising*, originally published in 1955, is also welcome. Like Pakenham it fits the Rising too neatly into a series of military engagements, each of which is dealt with very briefly, but, like Musgrave, he includes a great deal of documentary evidence throughout the text and in a series of still valuable appendices. Dated as regards context and simplistic in analysis, its enduring value is in engaging the reader with sources rather than speculation.

In his valuable 'foreword' to the 'new fourth edition' (i.e. the 3rd edition, plus items deleted from the 1st and 2nd editions) of Musgrave's *Memoirs of the different rebellions in Ireland* (1st ed., 1801) David Dickson points out that only 3 per cent of its text deals with Antrim and Down. Reflecting the sense of threat and siege that dominated his minor gentry class in West Waterford/South Tipperary in the decades before 1798, Musgrave's is, notoriously an ultra-Ascendancy and sectarian interpretation, linking 1798 to 1641 and the potent Protestant myth of mass extermination by Catholics, and was designed to undermine the continued campaign for Catholic Emancipation after the Union. In recent years, however, it has also been recognised more and more as a major source, with its vast accumulation of documents, some unavailable elsewhere. It is also increasingly recognised that, discounting the predictable regular eruptions of anti-Catholic prejudice, Musgrave was often an astute commentator. This new edition by Myers and McKnight is, therefore, a major publishing event, particularly given its elaborate index, making it for the first time 'truly accessible to the local historian and the genealogist'.

Musgrave's vast tome is also a reminder of the fact that while loyalist or Protestant accounts vastly outnumber those from the rebel side, yet there has also been a tendency to discount loyalist narratives as *simply* sectarian, or formulaic, or to treat them almost as if Musgrave had *written* rather than happily seized on them. It is, therefore, good to see an excellent paper on the narratives of Wexford Protestant women by John D. Beatty in the most original new publication on the rebellion to date (and covering all the main theatres of operation), *The Women of 1798*, edited by Dáire Keogh and Nicholas Furlong. While rather lacking in the insights of modern feminist scholarship, it offers an excellent antidote to mainstream history and the (male) fantasies of 'Comóradh '98'. In particular, Nancy Curtin's sympathetic account of Matilda Tone's 'virtuous republican femininity', Thomas

Bartlett's pioneering and sensitive use of 'female evidences in courts martial' to illuminate not just their role in the rebellion but their wider social role, and Kevin O'Neill's outstanding analysis of the Quaker radicalism of Mary Shackleton Leadbetter, make major contributions and signal new research. Until the still largely 'hidden Ireland' of rural popular culture is tackled in the same way, and neglected Gaelic and folklore sources systematically examined, we will remain largely ignorant of what is still the great unanswered question about 1798, especially in Wexford; 'what motivated the extraordinary courage, and sometimes equally extraordinary cruelty of the rebel rank and file? It is regrettable that in this bicentenary year they should still be patronised as mere extensions and mouthpieces of the bourgeois United Irish leadership and as pawns in contemporary political agendas.

Notes and References

1 Colm Tóibín, 'New ways of killing your father', *London Review of Books*, 18 November 1993, p. 3.

2 T. Dunne, 'Wexford's "Comóradh '98": politics, heritage and history', in *History Ireland* (forthcoming, Summer 1998).

3 L.M. Cullen, *The Emergence of Modern Ireland* (London, 1981); 'The 1798 rebellion in its eighteenth century context', in P.J. Corish (ed.), *Radicals, Rebels and Establishments* (Belfast, 1985), pp. 91-113; 'The 1798 rebellion in Wexford: United Irish organisation, membership, leadership', in K. Whelan (ed.), *Wexford: history and society* (1987), pp. 248-95.

4 K. Whelan, 'The role of the Catholic priest in the 1798 rebellion in County Wexford', in K. Whelan (ed.), *Wexford: history and society*, pp. 296-315; 'The religious factor in the 1798 rebellion in County Wexford', in P. O'Flanagan, P. Ferguson and K. Whelan (eds), *Rural Ireland 1600–1900: modernisation and change* (Cork, 1987), pp. 62-85.

5 *Memoirs of Miles Byrne* (Paris and New York, 1863: I.U.P. reprint, Shannon, 1972), vol. I, pp. 53, 61, 66, 194, 239-40.

6 K. Whelan, 'Politicisation in County Wexford and the origins of the 1798 rebellion', in D. Dickson and H. Gough (eds), *Ireland and the French Revolution* (1990), pp. 156-178.

7 T. Dunne, '1798: memory, history, commemoration', *Journal of the Wexford Historical Society*, No. 16, (1996-7), pp. 5-39.

Braveheart: Raising the Stakes of History[1]

WILLY MALEY

Mel Gibson (b. Peekshill, New York, emigrated to Australia in 1968, five feet and ten inches in height) to play Sir William Wallace (b.1270?, Elderslie, Scotland, six feet and seven inches in height) in a film financed from institutional investors in America and shot on location primarily in Ireland. At last Scottish cultural nationalism has left the kailyard behind, embracing fully the post-industrial world and the glob-alisation of ethnicity! (Graeme Morton)

SHORT SOLDIER: William Wallace is 7 feet tall.

WILLIAM: Yes, I've heard. Kills men by the hundreds, and if he were here he'd consume the English with fireballs from his eyes and bolts of lightning from his arse. I am William Wallace, and I see before me an army of my countrymen here in defiance of tyranny. You have come to fight as free men, and free men you are. What would you do without freedom? Will you fight?

TALL SOLDIER: Fight against that? No, we will run, and we will live.

WILLIAM: Aye, fight and you may die, run and you'll live. At least a while. And dying in your beds many years from now, would you be willing to trade all the days from this day to that for one chance, just one chance to come back here and tell our enemies that they may take our lives, but they'll never take our freedom.

(Randall Wallace, *Braveheart*)

Screenwriter Randall Wallace and his wife were on vacation in Edinburgh when he glimpsed a statue of William Wallace and learned some of the legends about him. He began to research and discovered that *beyond the preponderance of legends, very few actual facts are known about*

> *him*. His work on the screenplay for *Braveheart* commenced after reading a 1740 English translation of rhyming Scottish verse presenting legends about Wallace.
>
> (*Braveheart* Production Notes; emphasis added)

> 'History is impressionistic', says Randall Wallace. 'What William Wallace did can be inferred from the passion of his supporters and the hatred of his enemies. The great legends about him built a fire in my heart. His life communicated that you will prevail if you are faithful to what you believe in; and if those you love believe in you. Your body can be broken but not your spirit'. When the writer is asked if he might be a descendant of William Wallace, he replies, 'I don't know in fact, but in spirit I am – and spirit is greater than fact'.
>
> (*Braveheart* Production Notes)

Introduction

Excuse me if I initially adopt the confessional mode, and divulge some relevant autobiographical details. I have the feeling of being on the scaffold, and I'm not sure whether I'll be calling for mercy or freedom by the end of this torture. I'm neither a medieval historian nor a film critic by profession. (The two qualifications don't often converge, I imagine, though medieval historians appear not to have resisted the urge to comment on the depiction of their area of study on the big screen, while film critics have been equally quick to denounce *Braveheart* as historically inaccurate, assuming an expertise that is perhaps problematic.) Being neither, I can't claim to be both. My chief research interests are in sixteenth- and seventeenth-century literature, and in contemporary theory, particularly postcolonialism and deconstruction. My work on the Renaissance has begun to touch on the interaction of Scottish and Irish culture and identity in that period, *vis-à-vis* England, and this is something that is treated in *Braveheart*, however fleetingly and frivolously, and which I'd like to speak very briefly about, but first, I hope you'll forgive me if I begin anecdotally. History is at root, like film, a form of storytelling that necessarily includes legend and anecdote, hearsay and heresy, fiction as well as fact.

Facing up to national identity – and history, the two things being closely linked – takes a brave heart. In the summer of 1995, having found myself with an afternoon to kill in Bristol, in England, on my way back to Glasgow, I elected to see, not Bruce and Wallace, but Bruce Willis in his latest blockbuster, *Die Hard with a Vengeance* – a film, incidentally, very much concerned with ethnicity and national identity, concerned, in fact, with the displaced violence that is the legacy of national reunification, in this case German. In the event, making my way to my seat in the dark, I stumbled a couple of times and said something in my best English like 'Gonnae get oot ma road'. Once seated, the advertisements began, followed by trailers for forthcoming attractions.

Suddenly, Mel Gibson's face, painted blue, filled the screen – I hadn't seen anything quite like this since the European Championships in Sweden back in 1992 – and he cried:

> 'Would you be willing to trade all the days from this day to that for one chance, just one chance [that's two chances] to tell our enemies that they may take our lives [I thought he said wives] but they will never take our freedom!'

At this point, several heads turned to look at me, perhaps to make sure that I wasn't Mel Gibson, in for a sneak preview of audience reaction but more likely to see what my response might be. I did hear someone say 'He looks the part', but I'm not sure if this was directed at Mel or Maley. By this time, my face red and filling the cinema, I had sunk so far into my seat as to be barely visible, but I could just make out a horde of kilted warriors charging towards me, claymores raised. Not a pretty sight. My embarrassment and confusion was intensified by the fact that I recognised some of those individuals as hitherto unemployed actors with whom I was acquainted in Glasgow. I felt very alienated. Here I was, out of my country – out of my period too, in what was for me an exemplary cosmopolitan setting, and I had been fixed, interpellated in discourse, in proper Althusserian fashion, despite myself, no longer, as I had fondly imagined, the self-generating originator of my own identity. I was discovered. Recognised as one of *them*. Being – subjectively – in denial of nationalism doesn't preclude being implicated. As Althusser would put it, ideology actually depends upon convincing its subjects that they are outside of it – outside of, for example, nationalism and violence. This fantasy – of being outside – is a necessary prerequisite for the successful operation of ideology. Imagining yourself to be a neutral, classless, sexless, ahistorical subject is arguably easier in academe than elsewhere, but it involves a certain amount of self-delusion. You may very well think yourself invisible, objective, unobtrusive – others are harder to persuade. The voice might give you away – the phrase going before the content – saying something different from what was intended, saying for example: 'I'm working-class and therefore the very type of person likely to enjoy a film like *Braveheart*'. Accent affirms identity, it says 'yes' or 'aye', and never 'nay'. I remember a line from a Robert Mitchum film where a woman says: 'My, you're tall', and he replies:

'I didn't mean to be'. I didn't mean to be Scottish. It was an accident of birth, of history. Then again, as Longshanks complains: 'The trouble with Scotland is that it's full of Scots'.

Class, Nation, and Identity

After that initial brush with *Braveheart* in Bristol, it took me three months to get round to seeing the movie, but having held out for as long as I could I was finally driven by some rather disturbing reviews that seemed unhappy with Mel Gibson's ethnicity, and which focused on the film's alleged historical inaccuracy, as though it were a textbook: *The New History of Scotland* in ten volumes by Professor Randall Wallace, raised in Tennessee, starring the Australian-New York-Irish midget, the amazing Mel Gibson. Since openness to the other is quite an issue for me – as a first generation academic and professional from a lower working-class background – I found the anti-American streak in some reviews rather distasteful. The British Left has a long tradition of anti-Americanism that I find generally problematic. I also had the feeling that what was being attacked was a certain form of popular culture, the blockbuster, the box-office record breaker, the hugely successful cultural import. Harlan Kennedy's diatribe was typical of a certain journalistic response:

> We're acclaiming the moment when Aussie americanus went to the Highlands to paint his face blue, declare war on Limeyland, and bequeath the ultimate footnote to movie martyrology.[2]

Few critical reviews of the film actually focused on content or dialogue. A particularly vitriolic denunciation of the film by Colin McArthur concluded by declaring that if the 'film has any appeal to Scots it will be to the most regressively xenophobic among us'.[3] Leaving aside the vexed question of whether one could be progressively xenophobic, this piece and others like it acted for me as a magnet rather than a deterrent. If ever there was an invitation to attend a screening that was it. The sight of revisionism in full froth is indeed a wonder to behold.

By the time I saw *Braveheart*, on a weekday, in a half-full cinema, with no choruses of 'Flower of Scotland', with much passion spent, I was struck by the emotional force of hearing so many Scottish accents on screen, some of which, including Mel Gibson's, were much more 'authentic', to my ears at least, than anything available on TV or in lecture theatres, where the broadest brogues are confined to maintenance, security, and catering staff. I felt another kind of discomfort, not just embarrassment this time, or the recognition of seeing familiar faces, but recognition of another sort, of complicity and identification, however fraught and mediated by my civilising years in Cambridge and London. For me, the question of social class has always mattered more than any other form of affiliation, and I sensed that this was a film that was dividing people along class lines – as well as gender and race. Its uncompromising rebelliousness and anti-authoritarianism was directed, somewhat anachronistically, against an English government that spoke in received pronunciation, but directed, too, against a collaborative national bourgeoisie. I did not shelve my misgivings about the film, but I did modify my views in light of what I saw as a clear high versus low culture divide. I was also struck by the extent to which the film was self-critical, the degree to which it questioned its own historicity, the levels on which it conducted an internal debate. From the opening line there is a sense of contingency and provisionality in the story. We hear the voice of Robert the Bruce say: 'I shall tell you of William Wallace. Historians from England will say I am a liar, but history is written by those who have hanged heroes'.

Now, I'm not about to defend *Braveheart*. The film is big enough and ugly enough – and long enough – to take care of itself, and few people would want to condone its violence, homophobia, and misogyny, however powerful, passionate, and moving they found it as a piece of cinema. The model of militant masculinity that *Braveheart* promulgates is summed up in one of the film's most enduring images – the scene in which Wallace and his fellow warriors raise a row of stakes to thwart the approaching English heavy cavalry at the Battle of Stirling Bridge. Much of what has been said of the interplay of anglophobia and homophobia in *Braveheart* is sharp and eloquent, but as a film – and therefore as a text – it does raise some issues (if not a few stakes). *Braveheart* seems in fact to splice three dominant discourses of Scottishness that have been subject to severe criticism in this century – Tartanry, Kailyard, and Clydesideism – that is tourism, ruralism, and workerism. But it arguably elicits a fourth Scottish strain – Inferiorism, or the cultural cringe – witness my rolling up into a ball in that Bristol cinema. 'Inferiorism' – a term borrowed from Frantz Fanon – implies that one holds the symbols of one's national culture – always fantastical – in low esteem, due to the nation's subordinate position within a larger state. Anglocentric British superiorism depends upon Scottish inferiorism. An Anglo-Irish conspiracy of silence concerning Scotland could not survive without the complicity of that excluded third space, or *media natio*. My sense of culpability stems from the fact that for ten years I worked on English views of Ireland, in Cambridge and London, and it was only recently, upon my less-than-triumphant return to Scotland, that I began to see a problem with this work. Because of colonialism, and the effects it has on education, it is quite possible to go through the Scottish education system – at all levels – and learn little about Scottish history and culture. Looking back at my work on Spenser and Ireland, and on early modern English representations of Ireland in general, I can see just how much my cultural conditioning blinded me to the place of Scotland in Anglo-Irish history. Re-reading Spenser and Bacon and Milton I can see now how prevalent was Scotland in texts I'd hitherto regarded as being 'all about Ireland'.[4] I was helped in this prior ignorance of course by the English and anglocentric historiography to which I had recourse, but aided also by my own refusal to face up to 'my nation', even though each time I opened my mouth to deny it I flatly contradicted myself.

As a lapsed Scot, then, I suffered a relapse. As an act of atonement, penitence for my wasted youth, I've been fishing for Scotland in the troubled waters of the Irish works of those major canonical English authors who most interest me. Ultimately I know I have to dive in and do something Scottish – whatever that may be – but meanwhile part of my initial reparation is to chart the extent to which early modern texts previously read in an Anglo-Irish light can be placed firmly within a three-kingdom context.

For example, in *A View of the State of Ireland* Spenser recounts the invasion of Ireland in 1315 led by Edward Bruce, brother of Robert Bruce, King of Scotland. Irenius mentions in passing that the first person to declare himself king of all Ireland was Edward Bruce. Now, I'm not interested in the historical truth of this, only its political effects. Why should an English colonist assert the claim or record the investment, of Scotland in Ireland? But more to the point, how was it possible for so much of the criticism of Spenser and Ireland to blithely overlook Spenser's preoccupation with Scotland in that text?

Guilt is no bad thing. I think it was Woody Allen who said he didn't believe in God, but he felt guilty about it. I feel much the same way about Scotland. But one mustn't atone too much, or overcompensate, or hypercorrect. For the other side of the coin, complementing inferiorism, is superiorism, and perhaps there is a problem too with persistent patriotic claims to the effect that Scotland is more democratic, more European, more cultured, more philosophical, and so on, than it's rude southern neighbour.

Gayatri Spivak has spoken of postcolonialism as a 're-routing of the historical', and it may transpire that *Braveheart* is more of a postcolonial fiction than a piece of history, in which case those critics who have opposed it on historical grounds are to a large extent missing the point.[5] The film is about the here and now. Glasgow's *Evening Times* thundered: 'Mel Gibson plays fast and loose with Scottish history', as though every historian we have ever had has not done the same. In fact, even from the standpoint of history *Braveheart* is not as flawed as its detractors would suggest. Indeed, right from its opening line the film is highly self-conscious, if not paranoid, about its historical correctness. There is arguably a complexity in the film absent from many stock histories. Seán Duffy, who lectures in Medieval history at Trinity College, Dublin, has argued for the relative accuracy of the film in terms of its depiction of national politics and sentiment in the Middle Ages, not in terms of historical particulars, but in terms of its portrayal of Scottish resistance to English domination. 'Anglophobia was alive and well and living in medieval Scotland. Congratulations to *Braveheart* for a brave attempt at portraying it.'[6]

Duffy cites the Declaration of Arbroath (1320) in support of his argument:

> Take the following: 'For so long as there shall be but one hundred of us alive, we will never consent to subject ourselves to the dominion of the English. For it is not glory, it is not riches, but it is liberty alone that we fight and contend for, which no honest man will lose but with his life'. Who wrote that? Not some eighteenth-century romantic, not a Hollywood scriptwriter, but the men of Scotland in their Declaration of Arbroath sent to the Pope in 1320.[7]

The film is accused of being anglophobic but may more accurately be seen actively to counter hibernophobia and scotophobia. Those who suggest that nationalism of the type depicted in *Braveheart* is a modern phenomenon are slaves to their own periods. Any simplistic notion of 'history' can never do justice to a piece of cinema of this kind. Moreover, some of those most eager to refute the film for its historical errors assume that the medieval period – in which they have no expertise – is one that, uniquely, unlike any other, can be recovered accurately, wholly, unequivocally, as though history is not, in the first instance, about ideology and image rather than truth. In any case, no work of art exists merely to be condemned or condoned.

One of the film's historical sources is a long and inventive poem by Blind Harry that has been out of print for a hundred years, and has only now been issued in a fresh edition, thanks to the impetus provided by *Braveheart*.[8] That text, and subsequent manifestations, have created a myth of heroism and sacrifice that has been hard to dispel. In *The Prelude*, William Wordsworth speaks of his desire to record:

> How, in tyrannic times, some high-souled Man,
> Unnamed among the chronicles of Kings,
> Suffered in silence for truth's sake . . .
> How Wallace fought for Scotland, left the name

Of Wallace to be found, like the wild flower,
All over his dear country, left the deeds
Of Wallace, like a family of Ghosts,
To people the steep rocks and river banks,
Her natural sanctuaries, with a local soul
Of independence and stern liberty. (I.214-20)

These words were not penned by a Scot, expatriate or otherwise, but by an English cultural nationalist who did a lot for tourism. In citing Wallace as an example of suffering, independence and liberty, Wordsworth recognised the universal appeal of this historical figure. Far from having the 'power to enslave and impoverish imaginations', the story of Wallace has, historically, been the stuff of poetry, inspiring international narratives of resistance. It was exactly because it was a tale whose appeal went beyond Scots and Scotland that the film got made in the first place. It was Emile Zola who said he would 'always be on the side of the vanquished', and we would be naïve if we overlooked the fact, in speaking of *Braveheart*, that its global popularity lay in its status as a slave narrative, an epic of the underdog in the tradition of Spartacus. One of the things the film stands for – and the mythopoetic history of Wallace – is the struggle for liberty in the face of tyranny. That was what inspired Wordsworth. If the purpose of *Braveheart* was, as one critic put it, to 'wheedle money out of foreigners' – including the cost of a cinema ticket or video hire incurred by those Scots who were hitherto strangers to their own history – then the fact that those 'foreigners' can identify with Wallace suggests that more than Scottish liberty – or Scottish self-interest – is at stake. From Hollyrood to Hollywood via the Lake District there is a widespread identification with Wallace as an anti-authoritarian, anti-establishment figure, and a resolute enemy of tyranny. The Romantic Wallace – and also Wallace as a figure that haunts the landscape – is remarkably close to the Hollywood Wallace.

Aside from the question of history, there is the problem of representation. Many critics can be read as producing the very prejudices they seek to oppose; 'Mel Gibson is an Australian-Irish-American', in other words, foreigners out! Or 'the film was shot in Ireland', when in fact 20 weeks of a 26 week shoot was done in Ireland, and for tax reasons that say more about Scotland's subordinate status than any inauthenticity on the part of the production. Or, from Irish critics, 'The Scots are Brits anyway', which is true insofar as Scotland has had difficulty in asserting its own distinctiveness in a world where the terms 'England' and 'Britain' are used interchangeably, and where nobody has been especially keen to admit Scotland's place in Anglo-Irish history. Even postcolonialism, which manages to be the *bête noir* of revisionists and nationalists alike, insists on conflating English with British.

The film does not sit comfortably with any anglocentric view, including the binary thinking of the 'Anglo-Irish', where Scotland invariably gets lost in the hyphen of history. Modern Scottish historiography has not always recorded the interaction between Ireland and Scotland in a sympathetic way. *Braveheart* could be seen to address more bravely than have many historians the complex ways in which English, Scottish, and Irish identities interacted. After years of anti-Irish sentiment and resentment, it might be good for us to have some history Mel Gibson-style. In fact, in recent years, historians of the four nations that have historically formed the British state have been arguing for links between the respective countries, as against the traditional anglocentric or ethnocentric historiography.

Ireland plays a complex role in Scottish culture, often at the level of a vexing sub-text. While the 'outsider's' view (and even that of many 'insiders') may be that anti-English feeling – anglophobia – is the dominant expression of exclusivity or aggressive nationalist feeling in Scotland, religious discrimination – invariably boiling down to anti-Irishness – is arguably much more significant. There is a tendency in Scottish historiography to do one of two things. On the one hand, to ignore Ireland completely, except for occasional hand-wringing references to 'sectarianism', or to blame Ireland for what is bad or negative in Scotland. Generally, critics are more often inclined to compare Scotland to Quebec, Estonia, or Catalonia than to Ireland. Ireland is too close to 'home', too close for comfort. However, since the protracted peace process got underway, there has been a renewed concern with Scoto-Irish connections, which predate Union and Empire. The fact that Scotland and Ireland were at different times allied against England isn't always given adequate attention, and that's one feature of the film which, as someone who has worked on sixteenth-century relations between Scotland, Ireland and England, I found quite intriguing.

If one thing is clear in relation to the present state of Ireland, North and South, and with regard to Britain, it is that Scotland is on the agenda. What role a devolved – or even independent – Scotland will play in any future settlement remains to be seen. As I've said elsewhere, anything that breaks down the old Anglo-Irish binaries has to be a good thing. The so-called 'Irish Question' in its modern form is as much a Scottish problem as an English one. If anglocentrism on all sides has obscured that fact then perhaps it's time to open things up a little, to expand our concept of 'British' identity, for example, which is far less homogenous than some would like to think.

Implications and Consequences

Braveheart raises issues of gender, colonialism and nationalism that demand more than a cringe or acclaim. If it is homophobic and misogynist – and of course it is, no less than *Rob Roy*, or many other founding myths of nationhood – then it raises questions around the way in which the nation, and not just Scotland, is represented.[9] Film is a unique form in terms of its reach. A nation, if such a thing exists, needs recognition. Self-determination is never enough. Others have to be determined too, have to be accommodated and accommodating. *Braveheart*, content aside, has put Scotland on the map. Moreover, its anglophobia – if that's what it is – has found an eager audience in Australia, France, and South Africa, perhaps because anti-English feeling is notorious well beyond the bounds of Scotland. England has not confined its expansionist activities to its immediate environs. International recognition is crucial for any nation aspiring to statehood. Even if we accept that *Braveheart* is 'bad' history, then it is surely 'good' culture, part of a propaganda war, a battle for bravehearts and minds, 'good' insofar as it has opened up an interest in our past hitherto unfelt by many Scots. 'Braw' – meaning good – is one of the derivatives in Scots of 'brave'. (But brave itself comes from barbarous, and there is an anti-civility strand in the film that resonates with many national cultures reacting against the imposition of external authority or colonial rule in the name of civility.) If, in turning from the fiction of the film to the so-called facts of history, people find that others, besides Mel Gibson, have played fast and loose, then that can only help instil a properly critical attitude to the nation and its discontents.

Yet despite this upsurge of interest in matters Scottish, and in formal historical study, some scholars actually seem to fear that American cinema will supplant Scottish history books. As Graeme Morton puts it in his review of James Mackay's book, and others like it: 'The danger is blunt if credibility is lost: the Hollywood histories will become Scotland's histories. The video is, after all, often cheaper than the book.'[10] The question of readership, or audience, is crucial. Of course, every film and every history of Scotland is engaged in representing – that is, *reinventing* – the country. What Luke Gibbons says of *Michael Collins* could be said of *Braveheart*, that 'it forces us to reconsider not only the past, but also many of the platitudes which pass for political analysis in the present'.[11] One review of *Michael Collins* ventured that it was 'impossible to make a real history film'.[12] The story of Wallace is akin to that of Collins insofar as any semblance of historical truth is inevitably inflected in the switch from real to reel, but both forms, history and film, overlap and cross-refer. Keith Hopper's remarks on the risks of (mis)reading film as history are pertinent here:

> Discussing the merits of any historical film purely in terms of its fidelity to 'actual' history is a futile – if understandable – gesture. Too often this process degenerates into a simplistic search for obvious inaccuracies; a kind of historicist train-spotting which virtually ignores the created reality of the dramatic text by asserting the primacy of the written, historical text.[13]

Hopper rightly touches on the intertextuality implicit in cultural representations of political events, the textuality of history and the historicity of texts. At the heart of the controversies raging around *Braveheart* and *Michael Collins* is the question of how far our ideological implicatedness can be modified by appeals to objectivity or valulessness. It is a question of contamination, of the infectious nature and emotional power of artistic expressions of 'the Nation'. My own feeling is that we should no more condemn the film-makers for a lack of fact than we should condemn the historians for a lack of imagination. Indeed, historians might be grateful for an increased interest in courses in Scottish history. Ronan Bennett, speaking of the excitement generated in Ireland by the release of *Michael Collins*, points to a renewed interest in the past:

> I think the turn-out of extras says a lot about the appetite in Ireland for history. This is a live, contentious, dangerous history. And people have an appetite for it. The sanitised stuff that has from time to time appeared on screen hasn't satisfied those appetites.[14]

The appetite in Ireland, as in Scotland, may be for the dreamscapes of cinema and an escape from the nightmare of history. Some would say the problem in Ireland is that there has been a hunger for extra helpings of history, whereas in Scotland the reverse is the case. In Ireland, the story of Collins was common knowledge, however fractured and fragmented. In Scotland, the story of Wallace was almost entirely absent from the public sphere, and of immediate concern only to a few devoted scholars and nationalists. In *Braveheart*, Scotland has found a voice in an unlikely quarter, but one which, with all its faults, offers a richer modulation than the monotone of our erstwhile political and cultural leaders.

The Leader of the Scottish National Party, Alex Salmond, urged his members to take advantage of the emotional and ideological energy that *Braveheart* released, and to push further for independence. The rousing quotation with which I began was reproduced, with accompanying film still, on an SNP flier. Who knows, perhaps Mel Gibson, a New Yorker of Irish extraction raised in Australia will become the new patron saint of a separate Scotland. It's so easy to (both) laugh at this, and to tremble with fear – shades of Ronald Reagan (Gibson is no democrat, and indeed Scottish actors involved in the production have claimed that the film's homophobia reflected the director's attitude on set) – but when I was recognised in that cinema I did think about the ways in which international recognition of a nation, specifically, is often a necessary precondition of independence. Many working-class Scots undoubtedly found in Mel Gibson a new hero. Mel, in the best tradition of national heroic figures, has renounced this role. But the act of renunciation is no guarantee that one has taken the step beyond nationalism. 'I am not a nationalist' is a disclaimer that would have to be spoken in no language, not said at all, in order to mean anything, and even then silence would be another form of affirmation or false denial, condoning or contrarily conceding a commitment.

A film is like an accident. Every witness sees something different, something from their own perspective in terms of class, race, gender and generation. I believe there is something that can be salvaged from the wreckage of history, the wreckage of *Braveheart*. Two wrongs don't make a right, but in placing Scotland and Ireland side by side in conflict with England, albeit with Ireland appearing as the stage Irishman 'Stephen' (whose Caliban cry of 'It's my island' plugs into Wallace's struggle to reclaim Scotland), and Scotland as the stage Scot, the film arguably gets its history right, and suggests that the triple whammy of anglicisation, inferiorism, and anti-Irish sentiment can be addressed at a single stroke, and in an accessible manner. (In fact, the film teases the audience twice with the spectre of an Irish betrayal of Scottish interests, with Stephen's apparent attempt at assassinating Wallace – when he actually kills an assailant – and with the confrontation, then merging, of Irish troops seemingly on the side of the English but actually loyal to Stephen and to Scotland.) Hugh Kearney has identified the failure of the United Irishmen to persuade their Scots neighbours to offer them assistance:

> During the 1790s the United Irishmen urged the Scots to follow the example of earlier heroes, such as William Wallace, George Buchanan and Fletcher of Saltoun. But British unionism proved to be stronger than Scottish nationalism.[15]

Braveheart offers another 'take' on the Anglo-Scoto-Irish triptych, one which, however inadequate and clumsy, is paradoxically more layered than much traditional historiography. *Braveheart*, like *Michael Collins*, which sparked off a parallel debate between historians and critics of popular culture, 'is a film torn between the attraction of nostalgia and the imperatives of understanding the present through analysing the past'.[16]

Conclusion

I'd like to end with a quotation from the book of another major Scottish film, one that presents a no less controversial image of the nation, one that looks again at the unrepresented or the under-represented. This scene is lent impact in the screen adaptation by its setting within a bucolic – kail-yard (cabbage patch) – landscape, exemplary in its evocation of a timeless Scottish character. In Irvine Welsh's *Trainspotting*, the central character, Mark Renton, declares:

> It's nae good blamin it oan the English fir colonising us. Ah don't hate the English. They're just wankers. We are colonised by wankers. We can't even pick a decent, vibrant, healthy culture to be colonised by. No. We're ruled by effete arseholes. What does that make us? The lowest of the fuckin low, the scum of the earth. The most wretched, servile, miserable, pathetic trash that was ever shat into creation. I don't hate the English. They jist get oan wi the shite thuv goat. Ah hate the Scots.[17]

This defeatism or resignation is the other side of triumphalism. We find it in '1913' by Yeats, in Joyce's *Dubliners*, and in Edward Said's various lamentations on Arab capitulation. To shame 'the nation' into action is no different from spurring it on with a militant rhetoric.

Renton's speech is in the same tradition as the rousing oratory of Mel Gibson with which I began – a curious mixture of defiance and despair. Renton later remarks: 'Scotland takes drugs in psychic defence',[18] and this is reinforced in the last story of *Acid House*, where the main character comments: 'I think I'll stick to drugs to get me through the long dark night of late capitalism'.[19] Whether we're experiencing late capitalism, or whether a rather vibrant capitalism is going to get medieval on our asses, we have to find something better than heroin or heroism to get us through the long dark night.

Notes and References

1 This paper was first delivered at an international conference entitled Film/History/Culture, organised by the Cultural History Group at Aberdeen University, 26-28 August 1996. It was presented in a slightly modified form at the School of English, Queen's University, Belfast, on 13 November 1997. I am grateful to Professor Edna Longley for suggesting that I revise it again with a view to publication.

2 Harlan Kennedy, 'Kiltspotting: Highland Reels', *Film Comment* 32 (July/August 1996), p. 29.

3 Colin McArthur, '*Braveheart*', *Sight and Sound* 5 (1995), p. 45.

4 See my essay entitled 'The British Problem in Three Irish Tracts by Spenser, Bacon, and Milton', in Brendan Bradshaw and Peter Roberts (eds.), *British Identity and British Consciousness in the Making of the United Kingdom, 1533-1707* (1998), pp. 159-84.

5 Gayatri Chakravorty Spivak, *Outside in the Teaching Machine* (1993), p. 217.

6 Seán Duffy, '*Braveheart* . . . brave attempt', *History Ireland* (winter 1995), p. 6.

7 Duffy, '*Braveheart* . . . brave attempt', p. 5. For supporting evidence that *Braveheart* captures the mood of the period see Matthew P. McDiarmid and James A. C. Stevenson (eds.), *Barbour's Bruce*: '*A fredome is a noble thing!*', Vol. 1 (Edinburgh: Scottish Text Society, 1985). See also Diane Watt, 'Nationalism in Barbour's *Bruce*', *Parergon* n.s. 12, 1 (1994), pp. 89-107.

8 William Hamilton of Gilbertfield, *Blind Harry's Wallace* (1997). More recent biographies include James Fergusson, *William Wallace: Guardian of Scotland* (1938); Andrew Fisher, *William Wallace* (1986); D. J. Gray, *William Wallace: The King's Enemy* (1991); Peter Reese, *William Wallace: A Biography* (1996); and Glenn Telfer, *William Wallace: A Scots Life* (1995). See also James A. Mackay, *William Wallace: Braveheart* (1995). Before Randall Wallace decided to adapt it for Hollywood, the story of Wallace had been famously dramatised by the major Scottish poet Sydney Goodsir Smith, in a play called *The Wallace: A Triumph in Five Acts* (1960).

9 For an incisive critique of the film on these grounds see James R. Keller, 'Masculinity and Marginality in *Rob Roy* and *Braveheart*', *Journal of Popular Film and TV* 24 (1997), pp. 146-51. See also Luke Gibbons, 'Engendering the State: Narrative, Allegory, and *Michael Collins*', *Éire-Ireland* 31, 3-4 (1996), pp. 261-69, and Marilyn Reizbaum, 'Not a Crying Game: The Feminist Appeal: Nationalism, Feminism and the Contemporary Literatures of Scotland and Ireland', *Scotlands 2* (1994), pp. 31.

10 Graeme Morton, 'Review: Sir William Wallace and other tall stories (unlikely mostly)', *Scottish Affairs* 14 (1996), p. 115.

11 Luke Gibbons, 'Framing History: Neil Jordan's *Michael Collins', History Ireland* (Spring 1997), pp. 47-51.

12 Charles Townshend, '*Michael Collins', Sight and Sound* 6 (November 1996), p. 56.

13 Keith Hopper, '"Cat-Calls From the Cheap Seats": The Third Meaning of Neil Jordan's *Michael Collins', The Irish Review* 21 (1997), pp. 7-8.

14 Philip Todd, 'Interview with Ronan Bennett and Tom Paulin', *Sight and Sound* (December 1996), p. 31.

15 Hugh Kearney, 'Contested Idea of Nationhood, 1800-1995', *The Irish Review* 20 (1997), p. 7.

16 Ruth Barton, 'From History to Heritage: Some Recent Developments in Irish Cinema', *The Irish Review* 21 (1997), p. 55.

17 Irvine Welsh, *Trainspotting*, p. 78.

18 Welsh, *Trainspotting* (1993), p. 258.

19 Irvine Welsh, *Acid House* (1994), p. 240.

Ár nOidhreacht agus ár nArán Laethúil*

NEIL BUTTIMER

Úsáid acmhainní is ábhar do m'aiste. B'fhéidir go mba dheacair don léitheoir éinne ar coláisteánach é a chreidiúint ag trácht ar an dtéama seo. Tógadh raic ag an gCoiste um Chuntais Phoiblí de chuid an Oireachtais tamall ó shoin nuair a fuarthas amach cad a chaitheann na forais triú leibhéil ar an dtrealamh atá acu (*Irish Times* 27 Márta 1997). An aicme úd den lucht léinn is lú a samhlaítear an réadachas leo, áfach, d'áiteoinn go bhfuil siad chomh hábalta le haon ghrúpa eile ar a gcuid foghlama is ar a gcuid scileanna sainiúla a chur ag feidhmiú i slí stuama phraiticiúil, ach gur ar éigean atá siad chomh maith san as tar éis gach beart. Is de bharr na taithí a fuaireas-sa is a fuair mo chomhghleacaithe i gColáiste Ollscoile Chorcaí, go háirithe, ar fhostaíocht a chruthú i mbrainse an chultúir den ghéilleagar adeirim an méid úd. Ainneoin gur éirigh linn postanna a sholáthar, tá an tacaíocht ar a rabhamar ag braith go príomha d'fhonn spriocanna oibre a aimsiú tar éis trá. Teastaíonn uaim a thaispeáint nach sinne amháin atá chun deiridh leis seo, ach go bhfuil impleachtaí níos fairsinge le sonrú i gcás cailliúint mar é. Is gá tagairt do ghnéithe difriúla den bpolasaí poiblí chun an argóint úd a shoiléiriú go cruinn. Sula dtabharfaidh mé faoi, ba mhaith liom a rá nach chun aon phearsa ná aon eagras a lochtú atáim im chuntas. Níl uaim ach scéal a insint a chaitheann léas éigin solais ar na fadhbanna a thagann sa treis nuair a tugtar faoi shaíocht thraidisiúnta na hÉireann a ionramháil ar mhodh nár baineadh aon triail as puinn cheana.

An Oidhreacht agus an Oiliúint

Cuireadh *Diploma in Irish Heritage Management* ar siúl i mo choláiste féin i 1990 chun fostaíocht sa turasóireacht chultúrtha a bhaint amach do mhic léinn a raibh bunchéimeanna i léann na hÉireann acu in ábhair ar nós na Gaeilge, na Staire, na Seandálaíochta is an Cheoil. Ní mór na hoscailtí sna seanréimsí oibre – an mhúinteoireacht, mar shampla – a bhí sa tír dá leithéid sin de chéimithe i lár na n-ochtóidí. Ba é seo an tráth a raibh éigeandáil airgeadais sa Phoblacht agus an imirce go rábach ar fud na dúiche. Thart ar an am úd leis is ea a tosnaíodh ag ullmhú don Aontas Eorpach trí eiliminti lárnacha dár n-eacnamaíocht a neartú. Chuige seo, loirg an Rialtas moltaí ar institiúidí éagsúla sa Stát i dtaobh scéimeanna a cheapadh a bhfaighfí cúnamh ó Chistí Struchtúrtha na hEorpa dóibh lena gcur i gcrích. Mholas-sa d'údaráis UCC cúrsa iarchéime bliana a sholáthar do na scoláirí thuasluaite a thabharfadh traenáil dóibh sa bhainistíocht, san eacnamaíocht, sa chuntasaíocht agus i bhforbairt na hoidhreachta. Chuidigh eagraíochtaí ar nós FÁS, CERT agus Bord Fáilte leis an bplean a thabhairt chun críche, agus chuir comhairle orainn mar le tréimhsí taithí oibre a shocrú do mhic léinn, tréimhsí as a dtiocfadh postanna lánaimseartha chun cinn ar ball (féach mo pháipéar ar an *nDioplóma* i S. Browne (eag.), *Heritage and Tourism: the Second Conference on the Development of Heritage Attractions in Ireland* (Baile Átha Cliath 1992), Rannóg a 6 ['Education and Training for Visitor Attractions'], lgh 1-6, le haghaidh tuilleadh eolais ar an bpleanáil úd). Timpeall le cúigear mac léinn déag a bhí sa rang tosaigh, is tá thart ar an uimhir chéanna scoláirí i ndiaidh a bheith i ngach buíon ó shin i leith. Ba ghearr gur tharla forbairtí eile chomh maith, mar shampla nascanna Eorpacha faoi scéimeanna ERASMUS agus COMETT a cheadaigh malartú mac léinn agus foirne le coláistí sa Bhreatain is ar fud na Mór-Roinne (féach *ERASMUS and LINGUA Action II Directory 1991-92* (An Bhruiséal, 1992), lch 763, scéim darb uimhir ICP-91-UK-1285/04 agus clár imeachtaí Hibernia-UETP le haghaidh 1991-92).

Fuair cúrsa na hoidhreachta cúnamh airgid ó Chlár na nArd-Scileanna Teicniúla (Advanced Technical Skills [ATS]) de chuid Chiste Sóisialta na hEorpa (European Social Fund [ESF]) nuair a thosnaigh sé. De réir an chláir úd, maitheadh táillí an *Dioplóma* do mhic léinn, is ceadaíodh buiséad chun é a riaradh. £40,000 an tsuim a deonaíodh dúinn sa chéad bhliain (1990-91). Tá an chuma air seo gur scar sách mór é, agus gan dabht is sinne a bhí sásta an sórt san a theacht chughainn. Níor mhiste cuimhneamh ar na costais a bhí le glanadh, ámh, fiacha léachtóireachta dhá dhámh acadúla (na hEalaíona agus an Tráchtáil), aoichainteoirí ar saineolaithe iad a thabhairt go Corcaigh, agus acmhainní leabharlainne is oifige a sholáthar. Nuair is mó a bhí an t-éileamh agus an cúrsa á chur ar a bhonnaibh i gceart is ag fás, cad a tharla? Gearradh siar go rialta, bliain i ndiaidh bliana, ar ár bpríomhdheontas ón ATS, go dtí sa deireadh nach raibh aon phingin ag teacht ón bhfoinse sin faoi 1995. Tháinig stop leis an airgeadú san ainnneoin go raibh fostaíocht, idir fhostaíocht bhuan inphinsin agus phostanna fadtéarmacha lánaimseartha ar conradh, bainte amach ag os cionn dhá scór de chéimithe an *Dioplóma*, daoine a tháinig chugainn as gach cearn den tír, thuaidh is theas, is ón Eoraip féin. Ní thráchtaim ar na trí cinn de chomhdhálacha a reachtálamar i rith 1990-95 ná ar chéim M.A. i mBainistiú na hOidhreachta a tosnaíodh chun ligint dóibh siúd a raibh ard-cháilíochtaí bainte amach acu sa *Dioplóma* dul chun cinn breise a dhéanamh sa réimse seo.

Le linn dúinne a bheith ag cailliúint tacaíocht airgid, bhí cúrsaí i ngort na turasóireachta is an chultúir á gcur ar siúl i gcoláistí ar nós Mhá Nuad, in Ollscoil na Gaillimhe agus in Ollscoil Luimnigh. Fuair na cláracha nua san cúnamh airgid ón mbunfhoinse Eorpach chéanna ónar tharraingíomar an chéad lá (ATS/ESF). Cúrsa seanbhunaithe amháin, an *Diploma in Arts Administration* de chuid UCD, a bhí ar fáil le tamall roimh ár *nDioplóma* oidhreachta ach nár tugadh cabhair dó sna blianta luatha, chuidigh an ATS leis sin chomh maith ó lár na nóchaidí ar aghaidh. Ba dhóigh leat á léamh seo go bhfuilimid in éad leis na hinstitiúidí eile. Ní mar sin atá. Braithimse faoi mar a bheadh trua dóibh. Is cinnte go gcaithfidh na coláistí thuasluaite ana-dhua lena siollabais léinn is eile a fhorbairt faoi mar atá déanta againne anseo, agus i gcás UCD, mar a tharla le blianta fada anuas. Déarfainn nach bhfuil aon gheallúint faighte acu, ach oiread linne, go mairfidh an tacaíocht Eorpach atá ag sroichint chucu faoi láthair. Más fíor dom, cuimhnigh mar sin cé chomh guagach éiginnte is a fhéachann próiséas na hoiliúna i ngort na turasóireachta cultúrtha. Creidtear go forleathan go bhfuil an turasóireacht ar cheann de na brainsí is rathúla dár n-eacnamaíocht fara an tionsclaíocht is an fheirmeoireacht. Ba dheacair dom a cheapadh go gcuirfeadh ceachtar de dhá bhrainse eile den eacnamaíocht suas le leithéid an leithcheala san oideachas a bhaineann lena ndisciplín féin agus a thugann an tuairisc seo le fios is féidir a thabhairt faoi deara san oiliúint ghairmiúil oidhreachta.

An Phleanáil i gCúrsaí Oideachais

An bhfuil súil le feabhas a theacht ar an scéal seo? Níl aon deimhniú deifinídeach ann go dtarlóidh san, ar roinnt comharthaí sóirt a bhrath. I measc na gcomharthaí úd cuimhním sa chéad áit ar thuarascáil a ullmhaíodh don bhForas um Ard-Oideachas (Higher Education Authority). Tá teideal cuíosach fada uirthi: *A Comparative International Assessment of the Organisation, Management and Funding of University Research in Ireland and Europe* (1996). Chóirigh comhlacht comhairleoirí darb ainm The CIRCA Group Europe

Ltd. í, agus mar sin táthar ag glaoch *Tuairisc CIRCA* go hachomair anois uirthi. Mar a thabharfadh an bunteideal le fios, d'fhéach an cuntas le seasamh ollscolaíocht na hÉireann a shuíomh i gcomhthéacs idirnáisiúnta, agus cás na tíre seo a mheas ar bhonn na comparáide sin. I rannóg tosaigh an doiciméid ('Management Summary and Recommendations', lgh I-XVIII) agus i mír a §4 ansan go háirithe ('International Practices') liostáladh os cionn dosaen patrún tábhachtach i riaradh imeachtaí tríú leibhéil atá le sonrú ag fás sa tsaol lasmuigh. Seo é an naoú pointe díobh: 'Inter-university collaboration, multi-disciplinary and cross-departmental cooperation are developing apace everywhere. In many countries, governments and universities are taking specific measures to promote such collaboration.' (lch VII). I gcorp na tuairisce a leanann an Réamhrá úd deineann na comhairleoirí anailís ar gach coláiste sa tír, féachaint conas tá acu i leith na slata tomhais is fearr amuigh. Ar luadh ár gcúrsa oidhreachta i gCorcaigh mar sholaoid den gcineál comhoibrithe atá le feiscint thar lear? B'fhéidir gurb ionadh leis an léitheoir a fháil amach nár deineadh, ainneoin go gcomhlíonann an *Dioplóma* na coinníollacha a áiríodh thuas mar le bheith idirdhisciplíneach, idir-rannach agus idir-choláistiúil. Ní tagraítear ach oiread sa cháipéis chéanna dá mhacasamhla de chláracha léinn sna coláistí eile ná do na cúinsí inar fuineadh is ar fáisceadh iad siúd.

Ba é ba phríomhchúram do bhuíon CIRCA scrúdú a dhéanamh ar thaighde na n-ollscoileanna in Éirinn, chun tuairim a thabhairt den rath atá ar an scoláireacht sa tír seo. Mar seo a thug an comhlacht faoin bpictiúr úd a tharraingt (lgh 99-101). Aistí léannta a scríobh scoláirí atá ag obair abhus, chomhairigh siad an mó ceann acu ar deineadh tagairt dóibh i bhfoilseacháin idirnáisiúnta agus a bhí luaite i liosta a dhréachtaigh The Institute for Scientific Information (ISI). Admhaíodh go raibh teora leis an modh oibre úd: 'using ISI Journal titles as a classification tool appears to omit areas such as Celtic Studies where there are major strengths in Ireland' (lch 123). Is dóigh liom gur cheart impleachtaí an ráitis seo a scagadh níos mine chun toisí na bearna so i *Tuairisc CIRCA* a léiriú go cruinn. Níor áiriodh irisí ar nós *Éigse* nó *Celtica* nó *Ériu* sa chuntas, gan trácht ar *Zeitschrift für celtische Philologie* ná *Études Celtiques*, cuid acu ag teacht amach le céad bliain nó mar sin. Níor tugadh éachtaint ar irisí logánta cosúil le *Journal of the Cork Historical and Archaeological Society* nó *Seanchas Ard Mhacha*, ainneoin go gcuireann saineolaithe ón mBreatain, ón Eoraip, ó Mheiriceá Thuaidh is ón Astráil altanna ar fáil do na teidil úd. Ag cuimhneamh ar fhoilseacháin mar iad, níor mhiste ráiteas *Tuairisc CIRCA* a bheachtú mar a leanas. Ní hamháin go bhfuil cumas ar leith ionainn chun an Léinn Cheiltigh, déarfainnse gurb í an tír seo lárionad *domhanda* an léann Éireannaigh sa chéad áit.

Na hirisí idirnáisiúnta, náisiúnta agus áitiúla atá díreach luaite agam, is orthu-san agus ar an ábhar a fhaightear iontu atá an staidéar proifisiúnta ar ár gcultúr ag brath cuid mhaith. In éagmais na saothar san agus an taighde atá laistiar díobh, ar éigean ab fhéidir cúrsa mar *Dhioplóma* na hoidhreachta a thosnú in aon choláiste Éireannach. Is ionann gan aitheantas a thabhairt dóibh agus a rá nach bhfuil an scoláireacht úd ar siúl, geall leis, nó má tá, gur beag tábhacht is gá a shamhlú léi i ndeireadh báire. Tá gach seans ann go mbeidh tionchar substaintiúil ag *Tuairisc CIRCA* ar mhúnlú polasaithe i leith an taighde in Éirinn feasta. Mhol an doiciméad (agus ba mhaith an moladh é) go gcuirfí tús le ciste taighde sna daonnachtaí sa tír seo, ceann cosúil le The National Endowment for the Humanities na Stát Aontaithe b'fhéidir, toisc a laghad tacaíochta a fhaigheann na hábhair úd abhus (lgh XV, 222, 225-26). Má bhunaítear foras den gcineál san (agus táthar ag machnamh ar an scéal faoi láthair), an lú an maoiniú a gheobhaidh léann dúchais na hÉireann uaidh de bharr ionad fhírinneach an ghoirt sin a bheith á cheilt *de facto* sa *Tuairisc* féin?

Ag Cosaint an Chultúir

Fiú muna dtugtar aitheantas ceart do léann na hÉireann i *Tuairisc CIRCA*, ba dhóigh leat nach bhféadfaí neamhshuim a dhéanamh d'ábhar amháin de chuid na scoláireachta úd sa tír seo thar aon áit eile, is é sin an Ghaeilge. Tá seasamh ar leith ag an dteanga de réir Airteagal a 8 i mBunreacht na hÉireann (1937) faoi mar a bhí leis i 1922. Ach an mbeidh an stádas diongbháilte sin dlite di i gcónaí? Níor ghá a cheapadh go mbeidh, ar fhéachaint ar mholtaí Grúpa Aithbhreithnithe an Bhunreachta atá tar éis *Report of the Constitution Review Group* (May 1996) a eisiúint agus ar roinnt foilseachán eile dá shórt (níl aon teideal Gaeilge ar an ndoiciméad; tabharfar *Review Group Report* nó *Report* air thíos feasta). Bhunaigh an Rialtas an coiste seo i mí Aibreán 1995 chun scrúdú a dhéanamh ar an mBunreacht, féachaint ar cheart giotaí de a bhaint as, é a leasú nó a fhorbairt i bhfianaise a bhfuil tarluithe sa tír ó 1937 i leith. Ainmníodh cúigear déag le bheith ina mbaill den nGrúpa, ar a raibh dlíodóirí, lucht oideachais is riaracháin, ach is cosúil nach raibh aon saineolaí i gcúrsaí cultúrtha ná i gcúrsaí teanga *per se* ar an gcoiste. Ba é modh oibre a bhí acu anailís a dhéanamh ar gach mír ar leithligh den mBunreacht agus ansan a meon a nochtadh ina taobh. Tar éis dóibh an leagan Béarla (agus é siúd amháin) d'Airteagal a 8 a bhreacadh síos, seo a raibh le rá acu faoi: 'The designation of Irish as the national language is of little practical significance. The intention to give special recognition to the Irish language is understood and respected but it is arguable that this might be better achieved by including a positive provision in the Constitution to the effect that the State shall care for, and endeavour to protect the Irish language as a unique expression of Irish tradition and culture.' (*Review Group Report*, lch 15).

Is dóigh liom gurb éard atá sa mholadh seo ísliú gradaim don Ghaeilge, ísliú a bhraitear leis ar *First Progress Report* (April 1997) agus ar *Second Progress Report* (April 1997) de chuid Choiste Uile-Pháirtí an Oireachtais ar an mBunreacht atá tar éis dul i mbun obair athchóirithe den tsaghas céanna ó shin, ach a d'fhág diminsean na teanga ar lár leis go fóill. B'fhéidir chomh maith nár dhein an Grúpa Athbhreithnithe an teanga a scagadh sa tslí is cuimsithí de bharr réasúin áirithe amháin. Cuireadh srian leis an sórt fiosruithe a bhí ina gcumas a dhéanamh sa mhéid nár ceadaíodh dóibh Airteagail a 2 ná a 3 den mBunreacht a scrúdú. Is toisc go raibh sé ar intinn ag an Rialtas na haltanna úd a iniúchadh ar leithligh ar ball (*Review Group Report*, lgh iii, x), 'Because these Articles are central to the resolution of political relationships in Ireland, and between Ireland and Great Britain,' mar a measadh (*Report*, lch 10), a tharla san. Tá a leithéid ráite ar a shon go bhfuil an méid a leanas tugtha le fios mar leis an mBunreacht trí chéile i Réamhrá na tuairisce: 'The provisions of the Constitution are not wholly independent. There are inter-relationships which need to be taken into account when recommending change, and, particularly when change is finally decided upon and precise amendments are being drawn up' (*Report*, lch xi, § 10). Ar bhonn na gcomhcheangal idir míreanna éagsúla den mBunreacht agus idir an Bunreacht agus gnéithe eile den dlí lasmuigh den gcáipéis sin atá iontuigthe san abairt úd, mothaím gur dearmad é gan ceann a thógaint d'Airteagail a 2 agus a 3 le linn d'Airteagal a 8 a bheith á léirmheas.

Baineann na haltanna luatha san le líomatáistí fisiciúla na hÉireann a chinntiú (uimhir a 2) agus leis na socruithe is cóir a chur i bhfeidhm nó go ndéanfar na críocha Éireannacha a chomhtháthú in aon aonad polaitiúil amháin arís (uimhir a 3). Tógadh cás cáiliúil *McGimpsey v Ireland* (1990) faoi na hAirteagail sin lena fháil amach cén fheidhm a samhlaítear leo go baileach. Ba é cinneadh na hArd-Chúirte gur den riachtanas ('constitutional imperative') é athaontú na hÉireann a lorg (féach J. M. Kelly, *The Irish Constitution*, eag. G. Hogan agus G. White (1994), lgh 12-4). Níltear á mholadh a leithéid sin de chuspóir a bhaint amach nó gan a dhéanamh sa pháipéar seo. Is i dtoradh na breithe, chomh fada is a thuigimse mar thuatach é, atá mo spéis, go speisialta sa phrionsapal sin an 'riachtanais' i gcomhthéacs an náisiúin, nó maidir le heilimint éigin de shaol na tíre lena ngabhann an aidiacht 'náisiúnta'. Seo é an téarma atá a lua go díreach leis an nGaeilge in Airteagal a 8 ('Os í an Ghaeilge an teanga náisiúnta . . . ') san am i láthair, focal a ndúirt an Grúpa Aithbhreithnithe thuas faoi nach raibh aon dealramh praicticiúil leis. Más ceadmhach an breithiúnas a tugadh i gcás McGimpsey a thagairt d'Airteagal a 8, ráineodh go bhfuil coincheap an dualgais mar le freagracht an Stáit i leith na Gaeilge an-láidir go léir. Seans gur treise go mór an oibleagáid seo ná an cúram speisialta a mholann an Grúpa Aithbhreithnithe mar mhalairt téarmaíochta in Airteagal a 8. Ní chuige mo pháipéar ach chomh beag a chomhairliú do phobal na hÉireann conas is ceart vótáil i gcás reifrinn ar aon eilimint den mBunreacht. Má tá reifreann le reachtáil amach anseo faoina bhfuil i ndán do dhoiciméad 1937, ámh (agus is cosúil go bhfuil le linn don bpáipéar seo a bheith á dhréachtadh), ba mhaith ab fhiú a thuiscint go cruinn cad é go díreach a bhfuiltear á iarraidh ar lucht vótála toiliú leis.

Is chun poncanna a bhaineann le cúrsaí fostaíochta ina n-éilítear an Ghaeilge mar choinníoll oibre, nó na cearta atá ag saoránach cás a éisteacht i nGaeilge nó cros-cheistiú sa chéad teanga oifigiúil nó a leithéid, atá na cúirteanna i ndiaidh an t-alt seo a chíoradh go fóill (Kelly, lgh 53-60). Arbh fhéidir do cheisteanna níos scóipiúla teacht faoi scáth an Airteagail chéanna chomh maith? Cuirim i gcás na meáin ina bhfuil an Ghaeilge agus an cultúr a bhaineann léi chun coimeádta nó i dtaisce, nó na slite ina ndeintear í a fhorbairt nó a chur i láthair. Cuimhnímis siar ar an mhír dheiridh den aiste seo faoi *Thuairisc CIRCA*, cáipéis inar moladh gur cheart ciste a bhunú chun cabhrú le taighde sna daonnachtaí in Éirinn. Cén dualgas dáiríre a bheadh ar aon chiste Stáit, faoi Airteagal a 8 leasuithe, cuidiú le scoláireacht na Gaeilge ná le haon ghné eile de léann na hÉireann, an léann san a chuaigh ó aithne sa *Tuairisc* chéanna?

An Cultúr mar Acmhainn

Luaim scéal an Bhunreachta agus na Gaeilge mar gurb í an teanga an t-ábhar oidhreachta is treise a bhfuiltear á cosaint anois, b'fhéidir, i mbundlí na tíre. Má táthar chun baint dá seasamh san, cad eile atá slán nó i gcontúirt? Ráineodh gur sa Ghaeilge leis is mó a dhein an Stát infheistiú i dtéarmaí cultúrtha ó na fichidí i leith, agus gur san am i láthair atá a thoradh san le feiscint thar aon uair eile. Tá aird níos mó anois ná riamh uirthi go hidirnáisiúnta, chítear go leor eachtrannach ag teacht i leith á foghlaim nó ag blaiseadh de ghnéithe eile den gcultúr. Ar éigean a cheapfá go raibh na patrúin dea-mhéine ná eacnamúla seo le sonrú ar Pháipéar Bán an Rialtais um Ghnóthaí Eachtracha dar teideal *Challenges and Opportunities Abroad* (1996) a léamh. Saothar ceannródúil é seo ina bhfuil ráitis faoin tslándáil, faoi chomhoibriú i gcúrsaí forbartha sa tríú domhan agus mórán eile. Deir an rannóg dar teideal 'Cultural Relations' ann (lgh 309-17) go bhfuil an-ghaisce déanta ag Éireannaigh le gairid i gcúrsaí ceoil agus i ndéanamh scannán, ach ní luaitear an Ghaeilge in aon chor sa mhír úd, ainneoin na mbuntáistí atá luaite thuas. Seans nach aon iontas é sin, nuair a chuimhnítear gur tharraing an Páipéar Bán céanna ar an dtuarascáil deiridh dá dtagrófar san aiste seo, *Arts Plan 1995-97*, a dhréachtaigh An Chomhairle Ealaíon thar ceann an Roinn Ealaíon, Cultúir agus Gaeltachta (mar a tugtaí ar an Roinn sin san am). Is é a dúrthas sa cháipéis phleanála úd faoi chúrsaí litríochta agus na Gaeilge in éineacht: 'in spite of Aosdána and Arts Council bursaries, only 30-40 Irish writers are able to make a living from their work. Equally, it is difficult to identify a new young generation of creative writers in the Irish language. Although there are 10 literary magazines published in Irish and English, the Council acknowledges a dearth of high quality literary criticism. The Council would wish to stir the complacency which this might suggest, and to stimulate both more creative writing in Irish and a better critical perspective, essential to the maintenance of high standards' (lch 9).

Tá easpa tuisceana agus muiníne le brath ar na habairtí deiridh thuas ach go háirithe. Aisteach an rud é, tharlódh gurb shin iad an dá thréith is práinní nuair a bhítear ag iarraidh tionscnamh d'aon tsaghas, i ngort an chultúir ná in aon réimse eile, a chur ar aghaidh (féach Francis Fukuyama, *Trust: the Social Virtues and the Creation of Prosperity* (1995)). Chuamar i mbun na fiontraíochta i UCC nuair a dhíríomar ar an oidhreacht d'fhonn leas an phobail a dhéanamh ar an gcuma atá luaite ag tús na haiste. Tá súil agam nach maolófar ar na cúinsí a ligfidh dúinne, nó dár gcomhleacaithe ar fud na tíre, leanúint leis an obair atá tosnaithe, fiú má tá an bóthar giorraithe orainn ar uairibh cheana.

* Bunaithe ar léacht a tugadh ag an chomhdháil 'Heritage and Funding', UCC, Aibreán 1997.

Three Poems

(Translated from the Bosnian
by CHRIS AGEE)

MARKO VESOVIC

WHITE HAWTHORN IN PAPE

I

O, that blossoming hawthorn!
So effortlessly a king's crown
A cloud, a god even!

It sways. And does not sway.
And always, on the eve of Whitsuntide, it traces,
On the air, mysterious arabesques
Made of pure dream,
Gathering our looks, at least, round
The same ancient flame.

Its scent sweetens instead of God.
It smells the way a mother's foot might
Rock the cradle of a sick child.

II

It's been ages since it held the world in sway.
Yet the sun's eye will not burn away
All that issues from its rare
Shadow, still older than anything.
More despised now,
With the agitations of an exiled emperor,
Goose-pimpled in the breeze, it stands
Neither on this shore nor the other. A snake's
Skin is sometimes to be found
On its crown. Or some unknown
Songbird carried by rapt feathers
Beyond, or above, its flock.

Out of it, not even the devil would dare
Carve his fiddle, or a church's door-step –
        Still less a saint, a judge, a gallows
It secretes no healing balm.
Yet its thorn looks like a compass-needle
        Or the crabbed soul of an ancestor.

III

That one-storey tree.
Its sweep is not skywards, but downwards:
        It wants, first, to sink its fairy-roots deeper
Than the pickaxe can reach;
To breach the barren soil and lean the soul
        Against its soured secrets.
It's not a thirst shooting up,
But a growth towards the dead, spread sideways. And closer
and closer
        To our own house door.

It's not history.
Not even the real. Yet what boils in it
        Will never be driven out
By this flame, that bill-hook.
For isn't its every needle a guardian
        Of empyrean pledges?

IV

Isn't the hawthorn an hour of honey
That will not let the chaos in?
        A gemcutter that polishes precious stones
In the eye of the whirlwind of black powers?
Standing there like a messenger
        With a telegram bearing serious news –
For a whole lifetime, have I simply watched
With half-lidded pupils, threading on a black string
        The white pearl?

V

For our time and its
Do not cross; it is less
        Thisworldly after each blossoming.

Under the hawthorn's bark
The seraph is still asleep that after every flight
        Is closer to eternal youth
And the ever-burgeoning mystery.
O, that swan amongst trees
        Takes no notice of us.

But, at least, a grain of blueness that keeps watch
In every thorn banishes
        The ghosts of the midnight pillow

And washes the dross of evil off
Our words, bowls and blood;
        And everything under the sky, as on an anvil,
Becomes simple, and clean . . .

Pape: a small village in Montenegro, Vesovic's birthplace

GRAVE/CAVE

You, Arab script
You abound in sabres
And new Moons!

In the Ropushnjak cave
The dragons have vanished
But gone too is the treasure they slept on.

On this road, god knows when,
Barbarians cantered by on horses –

Look anywhere, and we're still choking
From the dust raised
By their hooves.

And the bat-like, hundred-eared
Child's soul is gone
That once heard the drift of padding
Snowflakes.

Are your petals, *world,* falling from this orange blossom?
Or is it just more and more shallow in me,
More and more illegible

Just as each day
These sabres, these new Moons
Are becoming less and less clear

On the crooked turban-stone?

SUMMA SUMMARIUM

The leaves of the ilex by the graveyard
Whisper prophetically.

And barley-corn ripens
Like those actors who
In the same role for a hundredth time
Stand forth before the audience.

Yet do not extol,
To the skies, your native land.
It ought to extol you.

Seen from this cloud
These meadows and fields
Are a stamp album;

And to the ant a smoke ring
Twirling from your cigarette
Is a whole new landscape!

And stop threatening for once
To return next time
To *this handful of land without history*
Only in the shape of a rider in bronze.

And before you leave
Stroke the bark of these trees
Which all the while have given you
Free lessons in standing tall!

These three poems appear in Chris Agee (ed.), *The Scar on the Stone: Contemporary Poetry from Bosnia* (Bloodaxe, Spring 1998).

Six Sonnets

CIARAN CARSON

THE POPPY BATTLE

She wore a bit of poppy between her teeth
Like a wound or a salve, while the ritual salt
Was spilled. The Civic Guards performed a somersault,
Then cleared their throats in salvo as she laid the wreath.

The former puppet languished in an unmarked grave.
I'd read about it in a powder magazine.
Light glittered on a detail of the architrave
In military hospitals that reeked of gangrene.

Red crepe fake felt paper poppy petals with their dot
Of laudanum in everybody's buttonhole
Exuded empty perfumes of forget-me-not.

I dreamed they had inhabited the planet Mars
With shell-shocked, pockmarked soldiers on a long parole:
Poppy the emblem of Peace and the Opium Wars.

SALT OF THE EARTH

'Nodding buds with four crumpled petals, showy red,
Orange or white flowers, exuding milky juice' –
Was this the Soldier, Red-rag, Cusk, or Poppy-head?
The Sleep-pap, or Fire-flout, Ceasefire or a Truce?

STC gazed at the page illuminated
By a candle as he sprinkled his thesaurus
Over it to see the words hallucinated
Into sentences. He felt like Sault at Tarsus.

Whole fields in Flanders and Kent are salted with them.
Good farmers do not like to see them in the corn,
And call them cankers, whose growth they find difficult to stem.

Children's eyes are dazzled by these Thunder-flowers;
Crumpled Coleridge took an age to be re-born –
Poppy the emblem of Death and the Special Powers.

ADELAIDE HALT

There is a smell of coal and iron. Black lumps
Of ballast gleam between the rained-on parallels.
I hear a blast of steam. Smoke floats across the dumps.
The platform trembles with the far-off decibels

Emitted by the almost imminent express.
Seventeen long coaches shimmered by to Dublin:
A blur of diners, drinkers, couples playing chess.
A sudden interim, then nitroglycerin

Booms from the quarry where they're mining basalt.
A gable wall says *Fuck the Pope.* I feel exposed,
As fragile as a model galleon carved from salt.

Overhead, the adenoidal honking of wild geese.
Adelaide? The name? A city or a girl, who knows?
There is a drink called Hope, a cigarette called Peace.

LIR

Next to Poppy in the Herbal is Potato,
Whose stalks and leaves and berries, like the Nightshades,
Are narcotic as the hemlock brewed by Plato;
Mashed-up, they make a pottage fit for renegades.

The tubers are not poisonous because they grow
Uninfluenced by light, which toxins seem to need.
Why, then, do I wander like a scarecrow
Blown by the autumn wind, like dandelion seed?

Our green fields have been sown with these Lion's Teeth,
Whose broken stems exude a bitter milky juice;
All Ireland has been turned into a blasted heath,

And coffins sail off daily to Amerikay,
As I do now, becoming this wild phantom goose,
Defeated by the wolfbane dawning into day.

WALLOP THE SPOT

One morning in May as I carelessly did stray
Across the wild Slieve Gallon braes, I met with Captain Rock,
Who did salute me on the banks of sweet Lough Neagh.
He wore a wig and high-heeled shoes, a poppy frock.

He opened up his Chinese box and offered me
A pinch of salt, some rare tobacco from his powder-horn.
Then he engaged me with the future history
Of Ireland free, of beauties waiting to be born.

He wore a spot upon his cheek, an earring in his nose.
The pupil of his eye was black with laudanum.
The last I seen of him was hanging on a gallows.

At a crossroads, with two other deviant brutes.
The next I heard of him, his skin was someone's drum,
His tibiae and humeri were Orange flutes.

MOUTH MUSIC

The Papists stole me then, and tried to make me play
Their Fenian music, but my loyal embouchure
Resisted them, and all the melodies of Moore.
I threw their Catholic legions into disarray.

My cardinal inquisitors were robed in red.
They touched their foxglove fingers to my empty holes.
They murmured prayers for the saving of their souls.
They read their Riot Act at me from A to Zed.

So then they built a bonefire for to burn me in,
Of broom, and bush, and willow, and potato flowers.
They bore me towards it on a purple palanquin.

As the flames roared around me, they heard a strange noise
Through all their chanting from their scarlet Book of Hours –
'Twas my ould self still whistlin' *The Protestant Boys.*

Two Poems

JUSTIN QUINN

HIGHLIGHTS

Last night the couple in the flat above us
Were in full flight: tirades and injured feelings
Swung back and forth for hours across the ceiling
Like bad jazz solos, long and repetitious.
Last week we caught crescendos from Sibelius.
And now tonight around eleven stealing
Through carpets and concrete slabs a wild, freewheeling
Moan of utter joy, which is their Anschluss.

But otherwise we'd never know they're there
And easily forget their sixth-floor sitcom.
We get on with our own lives – work and leisure,
Chores tending to our household appliances –
Which seem the same as theirs, that is, apart from
What happens between the highlights, in silence.

WEEKEND AWAY

This long weekend we're here in an apartment
Right in the centre, off St Stephen's Green,
Ten minutes walk from everything to clubs,
Museums, buskers, chain-stores, cinemas
And bars. The place was offered us by friends
Off west to Galway, to leave it all behind,
Their all to serve us as a hide-away.

Mornings have the seagulls wailing torment
Through empty weekend skies; they swoop, so keen
To see deep shoals. Their arcs have chimney-hubs.
A mile below them, awake and in amaze,
We have put to sea, are lifted high on fronds
Of waves, smashed downward, are lastly brined
And washed up on the bed beneath the duvet.

Beside us stands the Irish Permanent
Head office holding hordes behind a sheen
Of metal, glass and Brobdingnagian Chubbs –
The hoards of those who have, who can amass
Enough to build a home. But no ground-rents
Are paid at night by the hundreds that we find
Stretched out on pavements for a cider *soirée*.

A landscape on the wall to ornament
The living room. A Connemara scene
Of boreen, field and pole. Some fuchsia shrubs.
Black hills. Dark twilight. But something's gone amiss –
The twilight spreads beyond the frame, the fence,
Into the room and out beyond the blinds
Across the Dublin sky, across to Galway.

We hover in our spaceship, self-important,
Two floors above the brawls and shouts that mean
The bars have shut: *Up Ireland! Up the Dubs!*
Which fade towards two. We are anonymous,
Untouchable, looking on the street that wends
To Leeson's. Not a mugger stirs. And mind,
If he did, we'd lift off for the Milky Way.

With coffee and a bar of peppermint
You stretch out with your novel, the TV screen
Abandoned for Heathcliff running through the scrubs
Across the moors, his raging animus.
Another world inside these walls, which ends
And you drift all the long way back. Now bind
Your arms round me, your more real moorings, OK?

A different strand of hair is like a portent,
Licked round the inside of an otherwise clean
White oven dish (another in the tub's
Small plughole grille), a sign perhaps that someone's
Life, somebody else's life, will cleanse
This whole apartment space of us, in kind.
We buy a paper for each numbered day.

Two Poems

VONA GROARKE

INDOORS

I plunge the needle through and through
dipping, tacking, coming up again.
The ripple of thread that follows pins
out of its depth, a shallow hem.

I smooth the waves and calm the folds.
Then, to ensure an even flow,
I cast a line which runs from hook to hook
and pulls the net in overlapping pleats.

Which brings me to the point where I am
hanging a lake, by one shore, in my room,
to swell and billow between the light
and opaque, unruffled dark.

I step in. The room closes round me
and scarcely puckers when I move my limbs.
I step out. The path is darkened where I walk,
my shadow steaming off in all this sun.

THE SOUND-HOUSE

Small stones compose the wind.
Arranged just such-a-way,
so the edges whittle and

the gaps between them strain
the flow of air, in time,
they register its sweetest line.

This is the architecture of
a single note, pitched into
the movement of the wind.

Here is a coincidence of sound
which scales a silence
and plays two parts:

it orchestrates the wind,
unstopped, unheard;
the stones, dumb to the world.

Reviews

Discomposing Poets

Michael Allen (ed.). *New Casebooks: Seamus Heaney.* London: Macmillan, 1997. ISBN 0 333 60886 0. STG£11.50.

Peter McDonald. *Mistaken Identities: Poetry and Northern Ireland.* Oxford: Clarendon Press, 1997. ISBN 0 19 818422 0. STG£35.00.

'Hercules and Antaeus', Mark Patrick Hederman has written, 'represent two different kinds of poet: the first composes his own poetry; the second is composed by his own poetry.' Some third term would seem to be in order for a poet composed by his admirers, as Seamus Heaney is increasingly in danger of becoming. The Heaney bibliography has already reached daunting proportions, but amid the fodder of his post-Nobel acclaim few obvious landmarks stand out. Even the most gifted poets are seldom rewarded during their lifetimes with a book that not just confirms but enhances our sense of their total achievement (Hugh Kenner's *The Pound Era* is a rare example), and for all the fine critics who have written on him to date, such a tribute has yet to materialise for Heaney. In its absence, any amount of substitutes have been only too happy to fill the void. A festschrift issue of the *Harvard Review* recently offered us character references from some of the poet's students and even his bookseller, with scarcely a party-pooper in sight intent on anything so cold-blooded as actual criticism. Useful book-length studies have been written (Bernard O'Donoghue's *The Language of Seamus Heaney's Poetry* is exemplary), but much of the best writing on Heaney has come in the form of journal articles and reviews. Michael Allen's *New Casebook* collects fourteen of these written over a thirty-year period, as well as an essay by Heaney himself, and imposes itself at once as a lively antidote to the climate of pious and protective readings that has grown up around the poet.

The first of two contributions by Christopher Ricks, a 1966 review of *Death of a Naturalist*, shows us how far we have come since those balmy New Critical days. Ricks lingers fondly over an etymology here, applauds a metrical felicity there, and proclaims the Wordsworthian line alive and well. Of all the Heaneys on offer today, this is the least interesting: the neo-Romantic guarantor of an ordinary world, his Parnassian calm placing the squalid business of Northern Irish politics in its proper perspective. This position continues to have its advocates (John Carey springs to mind), but by the second essay here, Conor Cruise O'Brien's review of *North*, the critique has moved to more disputatious territory. O'Brien's forthright equation of Heaney's work with 'the tragedy of a people in a place: the Catholics of Northern Ireland' points to a difficulty explored at greater length by Peter McDonald in his *Mistaken Identities* – the unavoidable nature of confessional labels, even in the hands of critics concerned above all to move beyond them. The principal focus of polemic, as always, is *North*. O'Brien describes Heaney's relation to tragedy as 'fixed and pre-ordained' without developing the point, but for many critics the fixity of Heaney's tragic pose is precisely what is wrong with the book.

The parallels between Iron Age Jutland and contemporary Northern Ireland were always – at best – tenuous, but historical verisimilitude was never the point of Heaney's mythic method. Edna Longley's '"Inner Emigré" or "Artful Voyeur"? Seamus Heaney's *North*' remains a benchmark essay for its questioning of Heaney's presentation of violence as a ritualized inevitability. It also serves to remind us how much of the best Heaney criticism has been sceptical and even adversarial rather than meekly accepting in the manner of the *Harvard Review*. Longley's distrust of the 'area where literature and politics overlap', however, signals a belief in the discreteness of these two categories that has not weathered well. The main pressure on this position has come from the theoretical assault on New Critical orthodoxy, a theme which runs Heaney's poetry a close second for the editor's attention throughout this book. Its first stirrings can be seen in essays by Seamus Deane and Eamonn Hughes, and by the time we reach Thomas Docherty and David Lloyd the ascendancy of theory is complete.

Docherty's two essays, one a review of *The Government of the Tongue*, the other titled 'Ana-; or Postmodernism, Landscape, Seamus Heaney', bring an impressive array of contemporary French thought to bear on Heaney, not all of it noticeably relevant. In the second, Docherty invokes the trope of anamorphosis, a familiar example of which is the fishbone-shaped object in Holbein's *The Ambassadors* which, looked at from a certain angle, reveals itself as a human skull. His reading of 'The Grauballe Man' as exemplifying the condition of Deleuzo-Lyotardian future anteriority which describes 'the typically postmodern event' suggests a similarly oblique perspective. Behind the bluster of his borrowed theoretical poses, what is Docherty actually saying about Heaney's poetry? Old-style Modernists might fret over Heaney's trust in rootedness and the soil, but Docherty gives us a postmodern Heaney who reinvents his relationship with origins. Addicted to cinematic montage, this Heaney never merely returns to origins but engages in a 'process in "ana"' – analysis, anamnesis, anagogy and anamorphosis – which projects the past forward into an uncertain future. The argument is less than fully convincing, and frequently amounts to little more than Docherty's excuse for projecting Heaney onto whatever corner of postmodern theory happens to have caught his fancy. Thus two lines from 'The Grauballe Man' ('His hips are the ridge

/ and purse of a mussel') are held up as exemplary of the anamorphosis of gender, before leading on, via Luce Irigaray, to 'the drive towards the historicity of eventuality rather than [. . .] the fixity of a punctuality', Lyotard, Deleuze and St Augustine. All of which looks suspiciously like an admission that, with so many people to meet, postmodernism is having difficulties keeping its appointment with Seamus Heaney's poetry.

Of the force and intelligence of David Lloyd's critique there can be no doubt. His *Anomalous States* remains a pioneering work of postcolonial studies, with 'Pap for the Dispossessed: Seamus Heaney and the Poetics of Identity' (reproduced here) its most notorious chapter. English critics may continue to applaud Heaney for his vindication of the bourgeois subject, but for Lloyd this is of course what makes him so retrograde and pernicious. Lloyd's close readings of 'Digging', 'The Tollund Man' and 'Punishment' are excellent, but his pitch begins to rise worryingly in the final pages, as his strain of Marcusean Marxism builds to a comic conspiracy theory of Heaney the imperialist stooge. Heaney's work, we are told, shores up a practical critical aesthetic whose flattery of the individual reader (who doesn't exist anyway) is a deception 'conducted under the arbitration of an authority whose end is the constitution of a more integrated whole beyond divisions'. The conclusion is pure melodrama: the 'nominal decentralisation of literary production' represented by this 'minor Irish poet' is 'pre-programmed' to repress our awareness of the continuing meshing of Irish cultural nationalism in imperial ideology. That 'pre-programmed' has the authentic stamp of the Stalinist commissar, and is only the most conspicuous sign of Lloyd's failure to shake off his political unconscious long enough to come to terms with the reality of Heaney's work. The 'meshing' he condemns is evidently one form of postcolonial hybridity too far – for all Lloyd's repudiations of the humdrum monolithic self, his view of Heaney's poetry as contaminated by its English influences is every bit as underdeveloped as the purist nationalist position he claims to reject.

Docherty and Lloyd's contributions are worth singling out, as examples of the new orthodoxy which has come to replace Ricksian New Critical innocence. It favours disjunction and fragmentation of the subject at all costs (including the subject, in every sense of the word, of writing itself), though why these should be more radical than the continuities they replace is unclear. What is lost in the process is the belief in the centrality of poetry as a discourse answerable but irreducible to (say) postmodernist theory. In the rush to downsize writing to one more form of 'cultural practices', it is noteworthy that both Docherty's postmodernism and Lloyd's postcolonialism have little or no time for the aesthetic, a branch of philosophy whose stock has never been lower. And yet it was a Marxist, Adorno, who wrote one of the best twentieth-century contributions to aesthetic theory. A Marxist or postmodernist critique which did true justice to Heaney's poetry would make compelling reading, but neither Lloyd nor Docherty comes close. Of the more recent pieces it is only critics such as Patricia Coughlan and Richard Kirkland who strike a happier balance between the New Critical legacy and the opportunities of newer, theoretical approaches.

Michael Allen's notes to the essays are informative if more than a little nervous at times, flagging down references to 'English poets, Peter Redgrove and Robert Graves' in Ricks, though elsewhere assuming that introductions to Vološinov, Bakhtin and Saussure are superfluous. A petulant tone intrudes in his comments on Heaney's essay from *The Government of the Tongue*: 'Heaney must be aware that poststructuralists like Barthes and Foucault claim that authors don't matter' but, reactionary that he is, continues writing as if they did. It is also worth pointing out that, while the editor describes this *New Casebook* as a map of Heaney's reputation over the last thirty years, it is undeniably biased towards the contemporary: by the fifth essay (of fifteen) we have already reached 1990. Even so, there is little on *Seeing Things* and more understandably, next to nothing on *The Spirit Level*. But the Heaney of his last two books is a very different writer from the Heaney of *North*. There is a good deal of Parnassian in *The Spirit Level* but much too in the volume's best poems ('Two Lorries', 'Keeping Going', 'St Kevin and the Blackbird' and 'Postscript') that demands a newer critique than anything in the *New Casebook*. How critics react to the spiritual ambitions of the recent work will be of particular interest. Is there an intelligent middle ground between the credulities of the *Harvard Review* and David Lloyd's pre-programmed cynicism? The critic who finds it deserves to occupy a prominent position in the next Heaney *Casebook*.

In his *Negative Dialectics* Adorno assigns art the task of 'contradiction', which he describes as thinking 'the nonidentical under the aspect of identity'. For Adorno, the principle of identity serves to repress all that is incommensurable with the bourgeois subject. In art, the drive towards identity is manifested in the ideal of an autonomous artwork, against which Adorno champions artists such as Beckett and Kafka who attempt to give a form to the 'nonidentical'. Unlike David Lloyd though, Adorno was deeply pessimistic about our ability to move beyond identity-thinking, comparing the nonidentical to a no-man's-land into which we can make only occasional and perilous forays. His complicated relationship with identity-thinking is a feature he shares with a critic not normally associated with a theoretical stance, Peter McDonald. *Mistaken Identities*, subtitled, *Poetry and Northern Ireland*, begins with a quotation from the Opsahl report on the 'fragmentation of the old identities' and our failure 'to arrive at anything new which carries the same clarity'. The dilemma this encapsulates is never very far from the surface in the opening chapter or any of the six which follow.

A consequence of this failure is that Northern Irish poetry currently finds itself in a state of interregnum, to use a Gramscian term much favoured by Richard Kirkland, one of whose symptoms is our morbid interest in self-definition. Metaphors of grounding are central to Heaney's poetry, but for McDonald their use as tools of legitimation in Northern Irish cultural debate has been hardly short of disastrous; as it repeatedly proclaims, *Mistaken Identities* is an onslaught on criticism which would reduce Northern Irish poets to articulations of their religious and political identities. But there can be no question for McDonald of escaping the sway of origins (he freely adduces his own as a Belfast-born Presbyterian) for a Dochertyesque postmodern freeplay. His study of Louis MacNeice showed what can be gained from a reconstruction of origins too easily forgotten, and many useful pages of *Mistaken Identities* are spent rescuing and clarifying contexts for writers whose names are frequently invoked in the identity wars. McDonald devotes a chapter to MacHewdgers, as John Kerrigan recently called MacSpaunday's Ulster contemporaries. W. R. Rodgers' never-completed book of essays *The Character of Ireland* provides an interesting focus for its contributors' failure to run its phantom subject, 'the characteristics of Irishmen', to ground. What McDonald calls the 'fluffy patisserie' of Rodgers' sociable verse, Hewitt's regionalism, and MacNeice at his most drily journalistic are all obliged to admit defeat.

The space between Northern Irish poets' ambitions for 'identity' and the frustrating reality is not entirely barren however, and provides McDonald with some of his best insights. A chapter on 'Poetry, Narrative, and Violence' picks over the tendency in anti-revisionist critics like Deane and Lloyd to read violence as a narrative, capable of recuperation into meaning, just as, for Lloyd, 'the end of violence is [. . .] legitimate state formation'. McDonald is testy about critics who attack liberal squeamishness on this point but fail to acknowledge their own part in facilitating the evolution, in making it appear as inevitable as it does. He leans heavily (over heavily at times) on poems by Montague and Heaney in search of the moments where poetic language gives way to rhetorical pressures, reducing violence to a narrative coherence that McDonald sees as a preliminary for political oversimplification in the interests of one or other 'identity'. By contrast, the question 'Who exactly was he?' in a Ciaran Carson poem, 'Campaign', is horrifically answered when his killers 'took him to a waste-ground somewhere near the Horseshoe Bend, and told him / What he was' before shooting him. The sense of identity as something akin to a stigma, cruelly inflicted by friend and foe alike, is obviously more sympathetic to McDonald than the assertive young men we encounter in Montague's 'Paddy' and Heaney's 'The Toome Road'.

Few poets have resisted identity tagging as effectively as Paul Muldoon, the chapter on whom sees McDonald at his most enthusiastic. McDonald has criticised Clair Wills for an abstract use of the word 'form', the one thing poetic form can never be. His analysis of poems from *Prince of the Quotidian*, *Madoc* and other books merits high praise for the way in which it charts the mutation of Muldoon's stylistic templates under the extreme pressures of his subject matter. Muldoon's forms may bend but do not break: the exploded sestinas of 'Yarrow', for instance, are a subtle vehicle for the chaotically cross-cutting and repeating memories of which the poem is woven, while still managing to come full circle in its thirty-six line envoi. A chapter on 'Michael Longley's Homes' has less work to do attending to formal labyrinths and verbal pyrotechnics, but shows how Longley has managed to disengage his poetic 'homes' from the usual pathos of identity the word sparks off (Heaney's Tollund man 'Unhappy and at home' springs to mind, or Derek Mahon rhyming 'bomb' with 'what is meant by home'). McDonald is aware of the difficulties an Irish poet must face who refuses to play the identity game – any attempt to set Longley up as the representative poet of Ulster Protestant experience is firmly ruled out – but presents Longley's work as an exemplary rebuke to our expectations of what the proper business of Irish poetry is or should be.

Mistaken Identities has its shortcomings. It is disappointing that Medbh McGuckian merits no more than a single reference, for if any poet ranks beside Muldoon as someone who has flown the net of identity politics it is she. McDonald's tone, habitually pugnacious, sometimes shades into sourness and fruitless polemic. But in the end, for all the exasperation it provokes in him, McDonald is unwilling to jettison the concept of identity entirely. He continues to believe in the existence of a Northern Irish poetry essentially distinct from that of the Republic to the south, and the rest of British poetry to the east. He can do this by seeing it not as a model of self-conscious provincialism, but as 'the central, and critically defining, location for poetry in the closing decades of the century'. Its unique identity is simultaneously the best and worst aspect of Northern Irish poetry – not as momentous a finding as one might have hoped for perhaps. But no excuses need to be made for the dogged honesty and intelligence with which McDonald has sifted our thinking on identity for what is living and what is both futile and deadly. He is among our most conscientious critics, and *Mistaken Identities* deserves a wide readership.

DAVID WHEATLEY

National Fictions

James H. Murphy. *Catholic Fiction and Social Reality in Ireland, 1873-1922*. London: Greenwood Press, 1997. ISBN 0 313 30188 3. STG£43.95 hbk.

Gerry Smyth. *The Novel and the Nation: Studies in the New Irish Fiction*. London: Pluto Press, 1997. ISBN 0 7453 1220 9. STG£35.00 hbk; STG £11.99 pbk.

In the manner of Declan Kiberd's monumental *Inventing Ireland: The Literature of the Modern Nation* one is tempted to insert an 'interchapter' to bridge the historical gap between these two books. James H. Murphy's *Catholic Fiction and Social Reality in Ireland* concludes its analysis with the values of lower-middle class Catholic Ireland triumphant and with members of the southern Catholic intelligentsia either grimly entrenching themselves for the long battle ahead (a struggle which, according to both these books, will last forty years) or scurrying to catch the first available mail boat to Holyhead. Gerry Smyth's *The Novel and the Nation* begins its deliberations in the 1980s and locates itself within what he calls the 'new political, social and cultural languages' circulating through the island. In this, lower-middle class Catholic ideology is perceived, to use Raymond Williams's formulation, as classically residual and yet is still seen as capable of forming new alliances and taking fresh disguises. One can detect in both these works the occasional desire to voice the obituary for such values and yet both recognise that such an aspiration remains premature.

Catholic Fiction and Social Reality in Ireland is deliberate in its methodology and careful in its desire to keep the inherently disruptive energies of the novels under consideration securely fastened down. As the introduction states with telling bluntness, 'the principal aim of this book is to use an assessment of Irish Catholic fiction to explore the outlook of certain important classes in late nineteenth- and early twentieth-century Ireland'. One can wonder about the function of 'use' in this context just as the unproblematic opposition in the work's title between 'fiction' and 'reality' provokes a slight sense of unease; after all, as Smyth is careful to note, fiction is simultaneously both constituting and constitutive of class position. Murphy, however, restricts his analysis to fiction that 'both reflects the values and aspirations of the class in question and that was written by an author who was a member of that class' – criteria which might appear limiting until one encounters the vast number of astonishingly homogeneous novels that Murphy is able to marshal in support of his thesis. This is most evident in his consideration of upper-middle class Catholic fiction, and the work's analysis of the aspiration of this formation to achieve a state equivalent to respectable British Victorianism is revelatory. This prompts various speculations and, although it is beyond the stated aim of the book, it is a shame that Murphy does not consider some of the formal links and continuities between Catholic Irish fiction and the British Protestant cultural tradition. If nothing else, such analysis would further discredit what Smyth refers to in *The Novel and the Nation* as 'the post-colonial fairy-tale which tells of the Big Bad Wolf of English realism versus the playful, subversive, anti-realist nature of Irish story-telling'.

Central to Murphy's thesis is the rise of what he terms 'intelligentsia fiction'; a grouping that became prominent at the close of the nineteenth century and which inhabited the uncomfortably arid space between Catholic lower-middle class ideology and Catholic upper-class residual values. It is the opposition of the intelligentsia to the newly dominant lower-middle class that grants the formation its coherency but, with this, one wonders if the essentially reactionary nature of this project fully justifies the 'intelligentsia' tag. Rather than a politicised grouping affiliating itself to other classes with a conscious agenda of transformation, Murphy's collective appears much more diffuse in its aims and is typified by a tendency towards rebellious self-satisfaction. Murphy goes some way towards noting this characteristic in his consideration of Patrick MacGill's *Glenmornan* (1919) – a novel that features a character lamenting: 'If they [the people] were only educated, if they only read books, papers, anything'. In some ways however the insistence on this strict division between the lower-middle class and the intelligentsia leads to an impasse in that it underplays the inevitable negotiations and alliances that were forged between the two and therefore the essentially provisional nature of the latter's project.

Despite this reservation, the book is at its most engaging in its analysis of the cultural battle fought between these formations; a conflict which reaches its apotheosis in Joyce's *Portrait of the Artist as a Young Man* (1916). In this, the intelligentsia is either decisively routed or achieves a partial victory according to the length of the historical sweep considered. For example, while Dante in *Portrait of the Artist* is perceived as exultant in the crushing of Parnell and can damn Simon Dedalus and Casey as 'renegade Catholics', Murphy's book concludes with a teasing footnote suggesting the presence of a new alliance between the disgruntled though unbowed intelligentsia and the newly resurgent upper-middle class symbolised through the figure of Mary Robinson. The identification of this unlikely pincer movement is a fascinating speculation and one feels that Murphy has a great deal more to say on the various extensions of Catholic Ireland into cultural discourse. The book though largely resists this kind of analysis and restricts itself to telling what occasionally appears to be the slightly dour story of the inexorable transition from upper-middle class Catholic values to a lower-middle class state ideology. However, this of course remains a necessary piece of literary archaeology and one is grateful for Murphy's scholarly method and his willingness to chart a cultural trajectory that goes beyond the familiar narratives of the Anglo-Irish revival.

Smyth's *The Novel and the Nation* similarly expresses a distinct trajectory derived, in this instance, from its post-colonial theoretical apparatus but it is important to note that this concludes at a recognition of irreversible change. For this reason he is rightly scathing of the idea that the novel form has ever been able to function as a self-contained representation of society. Indeed, through the identification of the wide variety of fictional forms and voices found within the novels under consideration, the book takes a certain glee in proclaiming the death of the 'Irish novel' as a homogeneous object of study. However, for all this Smyth cannot resist a small gamble on what shape future Irish fiction might take and in the work of Roddy Doyle a diffuse tradition is seen to be inherited and encapsulated as Doyle, it is argued, writes the 'ongoing book of the nation'. This appears a slightly anomalous statement in light of the work's previously careful delineation of distinct cultural paradigms and throughout the lengthy consideration of Doyle's achievement a certain celebratory note is evident: *The Commitments* 'remains *true* to the world of late twentieth-century working class life' (emphasis added), *The Van* is 'very readable', while the technique of *The Woman Who Walked Into Doors* is compared favourably to that of 'modish postmodernists'. Such observations should not detract from the fact that Smyth's analysis of Doyle's work is original and perceptive but it is valid to compare such analysis to the more rigorous treatment he metes out to Northern Irish novels which are usually, as in the case of Eoin McNamee's *Resurrection Man*, perceived as in some way reactionary. This tends to be because they have not developed 'new languages and new perspectives' and have thus proved unable 'to break out of the orthodoxies which have fed and sustained the conflict'. Smyth's frustration with this state of affairs is understandable but this is one instance in which literary-critical prescription leads to a theoretical blind alley and in so doing questions the work's otherwise laudable instinct to avoid a simple sectarian division of the novels according to the cultural inheritance of their authors.

While I have concentrated here on two examples of how Smyth's theoretical framework is in some way exceeded by intruding discourses, such an approach reveals more fully the opportunities for re-reading suggested by the book as a whole. One important virtue of the concentration on narrative form that Smyth adopts is the manner in which it allows the Irish novel to be understood as central to (or exemplary within) the concept of a European tradition of fiction – a reading which compares to Murphy's habit of perceiving the Irish Catholic novel as an encapsulation of (sometimes bizarre) variations on a theme. Smyth's insistence on the post-colonial status of cultural production in Ireland is central to this as it provides a critical methodology dependent upon 'a complex set of negotiations between authorial intention, textual structure, reading context and audience resources'. While Smyth maintains that the readings of individual texts which follow this theoretical introduction are not 'slavish', they are typified by an impressive intellectual engagement which gives the work its interventionist momentum. Certainly the 'three problems of authorship' that Smyth identifies as central to the condition of the Irish novelist – 'special pleading, the reproduction of stereotypes, and the cycle of alienation and nostalgia' – are revealed as endlessly amorphous. This concentration suggests a certain weariness on Smyth's part. The book concludes with a consideration of 'the continuing insecurity and psychological dependence of "post-colonial" Ireland', an illness identified by the symptoms of 'self-obsession' and identitarianism (which, along with 'straightgeist', is one of the author's favourite words). Despite Smyth's attempts to suggest that the cultural uncertainty this leads to can have positive results, the fictive nostalgia for a more stable world it simultaneously engenders is not so easily dispelled. Perhaps in this way it can be argued that one of the functions of post-colonial criticism is to exorcise the monotonous oppositions on which it is based.

Read in sequence then these two very different texts illustrate the difficulty the Irish novel has had in articulating modes of cultural resistance. As Smyth notes perceptively: 'cultural nationalism appropriates the novel, compelling it to perform monologic ideological tasks for which, as an essentially dialogic form, it is fundamentally unsuited'. While, on one level, this awareness implicitly critiques literary-critical perceptions that there has been such a thing as the 'Irish novel' at all, it also reveals the textual ellipses and silences that are a concomitant aspect of such a totalising desire. It is this contradiction that both Smyth and Murphy return to repeatedly and the maps of inheritance and tradition that are drawn as a result are sophisticated and complex. However, if the novel is unable to embody the teleology of nation in anything like a satisfactory manner one wonders if the literary-critical text has evolved into a form much more fitted to the task. Both these texts are paradigmatic in this regard as they demonstrate the ability to encounter and assimilate diverse and disruptive discourses while maintaining a coherency appropriate to the status of that much-abused concept: the meta-narrative.

RICHARD KIRKLAND

Stars Get in Your Eyes

Ciaran Carson. *The Star Factory.* London: Granta Books 1997. ISBN 1 86207 0725. STG £13.99.

As an Ulster poet, Ciaran Carson is unique in a number of ways. He is, among the poets of the seventies' generation, uniquely bilingual, having grown up in an Irish-speaking household. He has a special place, too, in being foremost among those 'younger' poets from the nationalist tradition who have an urban, rather than a rural, background. Unlike Seamus Heaney or Paul Muldoon, he is a man not versed in country things: all that potentially enabling pastoral passed him by. He is unique, so far as I am aware, among that generation, in that he is a practising musician – a flute player – and he is a scholar of the musical tradition. He is further distinguished by writing, for the most part, in lines of extraordinary length under the influence of poets like the American O.K. Williams, at a time when minimalism, if not poetic anorexia, was the order of the day. Michael Longley has described these lines as horizontal haiku, which is precise, though it might be equally helpful to regard them as verbal sets of jigs and reels, because there is a sense in which Carson has sought an alternative enablement in the 'wink-and-elbow language of delight' that governs things like the 'session'.

The urban, bilingual and musical components of Carson's writing are distinguishing accidents of birth; the decision to write in long lines is a deliberate choice. It arrived after the pamphlet, *The Insular Celts* and his first volume, *The New Estate*. Unremarkable in the forms they contained, though those forms were handled with an impressive *élan*, these first two publications were remarkable for the precision of their language, the clarity of their thought and the spare coolness of their effects: the voice was restrained but not constrained. *The New Estate* was remarkable, again deliberately, among the slim volumes of its day for its inclusion of a series of illustrations of the founding of a great bell. There are, certainly, justifying references to the illustrations in the text, but it is clear that Carson took some delight in the serendipity of this actuality. That early delight in serendipity (the drunkenness of things being various) and in actualities (though the recent actualities have usually taken the form of long quotation from other works) have continued as features of Carson's work, both in the verse and in the prose. What is exciting about this, and Carson clearly realised it, is that what he inserted as illustrative text was not just quotation, but the thing itself; not just virtual, but reality.

After *The New Estate* there was a long hiatus. Then with *The Irish for No* and *Belfast Confetti*, it seemed that a new Carson had burst upon the scene – a poet who would weave elaborate and scintillating visions of the potentially nightmarish trappings of Belfast life. Detail spiralled upon ambivalent detail, providing simultaneously the perceived confusion and the stays against it. Carson's new-found ability to flood his singing lines with artefact, accident and incident, to keep control of it all and to forge a seemingly effortless polyphony from what would in lesser hands have been a generous cacophony was both inspired and inspiring.

The stays against confusion were provided by Carson's extraordinary gift for lighting upon the humane, the universal, the comforting common experience we had forgotten we remembered among the ubiquitous and threatening dilapidation and deterioration of this particular urban sprawl. The child in the sick room seeing the world anew through the yellow cellophane of the Lucozade bottle; someone repeating a word so often in his head that the sound blurs and reverses and the word begins to take on a whole new meaning: both are images of games, of idling time away, but also of what the poet does. This humane vision is saved from the sentimental by Carson's copious sense of the absurd. There *is* no Irish for 'No'; in a poem in *Belfast Confeti* the 'T' and 'r' of Terminus boutique have gone missing, as such letters incontrovertibly do, leaving us with a bizarre 'e minus'. There's no doubting the authenticity of this serendipitous observation, nor the scope for elaboration it gives. It's about a world where words are physically omnipresent actualities, and strikingly liable to corruption and urban degeneration even by the elements.

The persona in the poems is decidedly enigmatic, both included and excluded by the various 'wink and elbow' languages that surround him. He is *au fait* enough with each separate code to savour it, but no particular code is native enough to him to contain or define him. The words that each code uses are familiar, which makes each language seem inclusive, but the uses to which they are put are at best ambiguous, at least purposefully exclusive, and at worst potentially malevolent to those outside the cabal. The persona hovers cunningly in the, once more enabling, no-man's land, exploiting the ambiguity of his inexact location. Does he know more or less than he's letting on? We just don't know. We're not meant to know. Guessing is part of the game.

The fruitfully indeterminate standpoint is not something Carson's prose works afford him with ease. In the short articles he had published Carson had shown himself a writer of lucidity, charm and knowledge and his, literally, slim guide to Irish music from Appletree was one of those unexpected joys that make writing worth reading. It did exactly what it set out to do – to explain the rudiments of Irish folk music – but it referred, without obvious impertinence, to all sorts of unrelated areas of life. That is, of course, the supreme gift of the storyteller and, in fact, of the real intellectual, and it's the essence of 'crack' – the only spelling with which I feel comfortable. To make his writing 'crack' is, rightly, important to Carson.

The joy of the Appletree guide was to watch its writer bend and break the rules of guidebook writing as he went along, and to share in the delights of his subversion. In *Last Night's Fun* the meditation on the tradition was always intended to be completely subjective, which made such subversiveness difficult, if not impossible. And the book's premise was that the unwritten laws and conventions of the 'session' are simply not explicable. In the words of the Incredible String Band – the what? – the outsider might know all the words and master the tune, but would never quite learn the song. That premise is easy to accept, but its effect is to deny the author his accustomed and fecund position in no man's land. In order to write about that closed society he must come clean. He must own up to being part of the cabal, and certain readers are bound to feel excluded. But any book is an attempt at a partial sharing of an exclusive world – the author's vision – and Carson's avowed intention is to make it as much like crack as he can. That's the challenge – to maintain the illusion that it's all spontaneous, all inevitable, all just pouring out, and yet that there's some coherent vision, some intelligible but complex invisible guiding principle to which it all conforms.

Carson's most recent prose work has a title which any writer would have given an arm to have spotted: *The Star Factory*. Not thought of, but spotted – an actuality. Again the subject gives him little scope for the subversions of the poems. It's an idiosyncratic autobiographical piece, ambitious to combine pure reminiscence – his relationship with his father, school friendships, the Belfast that is gone, if it ever existed – with actualities and meditations which map the poet's mind: the way one word leads to another word, the way he thinks of something else, and something else again. To some extent one can understand Germaine Greer's passionately expressed criticism of it as some form of self-abuse, but surely she was missing the point. Carson is much too good a writer not to have been aware that to include huge chunks from reference books, the whole of an essay a schoolboy had sent to him, his own preface to another book, endless dubious footnotes and endless lists, to break in to his own narrative with something that was actually happening in the room, might annoy the reader. Surely it's meant to. It's meant to make you question what you're reading and why, how you read it and why, how it was written and why. That's a risky business, and clearly it didn't work for Germaine, but I suspect that though she didn't enjoy this particular exploration of the mind that does it, she'd be beguiled by the poems it produces.

LEON McAULEY

Purity and Dirt

Trevor Joyce. *Syzygy*. Bray: Wild Honey Press, 1998, distributed by Hardpressed Poetry, Dublin. IR£3.50.

One useful point of entry into Trevor Joyce's challenging new sequence, *Syzygy*, is 'Chimera', from his 1995 collection *stone floods*. The polyphonic 'Chimera' conjoins dialogically Richard Lovelace's self-satisfied, urbane wit, Aloysius Bertrand's apocalyptic forebodings of the levelling of all bounds, and the Book of Lieh Tze's acceptance of the provisionality of limits in nature, the fragility of the ego and the interconnected diversity of the phenomenal world. While Lovelace's verbal ingenuity and Bertrand's nausea are aspects of Joyce's writing from *Pentahedron* (1972) on, it is the concerns of the Book of Lieh Tze which chime most fully with those of his recent poetry, including *Syzygy*. Furthermore, the complex structure of the two interlaced parts of *Syzygy* recalls even as it excels the earlier poem's utilisation of the Japanese *renga* form, the latter employing, in the words of Joyce's note to the poem, 'systematic ambiguity to chain together a series of brief stanzas every one of which hinges both forward and backward'. In the case of *Syzygy*, systematic ambiguity derives, not from a literary precedent, but from the method of composition described in Joyce's annotations to the sequence. In brief, the 'palindromic net', as Joyce felicitously terms it, is achieved by means of a base text, now fossilised in the second part of the sequence, that dictates the opening and closing segments of each of the twelve units or 'cells' of part I. Once those cells are complete, their material, mediated through the controlling procedures, determines the remainder of part II. Space prevents a more elaborate exposition of the text's structure: the interested reader can consult Joyce's notes for a detailed commentary. Of greater importance, I feel, are the implications of this method of composition for our response to and evaluation of this text. Its formal discipline lies in the manner in which the originating lines prescribe, to an extent, the remainder of the text. This approach, of course, is not unique to Joyce: John Cage's famous mesostic texts, his 'writing through' of others' works, are generated in a not unrelated fashion to *Syzygy*. Even in the context of recent Irish poetry such avant-gardism finds a few – though only a few – parallels: Randolph Healy's *Flame* (1997), also published by Wild Honey Press, is likewise constructed using chance procedures. In Joyce's case, the partially prescripted nature of the sequence is at one with Joyce's recurrent preoccupation, from *Pentahedron* to *stone floods*, with bounds, order and, crucially, with their breakdown and transgression. For, as Joyce's notes confess, the symmetry of the sequence is not absolute, there is a tiny flaw in the crystalline structure; and it is precisely this alloyment that brings the formal qualities of *Syzygy* into alignment with its thematic concern: the relationship between conceptual order and the particularity of the phenomenal world. In a manner reminiscent of Adorno, the text views the former as necessary and inescapable, but stifling and ineluctably involved with other, harsher kinds of domination:

> when the thieving
> that was well advanced faltered
> the imperial presence surveyed
> the ordered territories
> and declared in measured words
> nothing there is savage any more
> intelligence and griefs are tamed
> rage is reduced in parks
> only perhaps along the furthest bounds
> may be some dirt a little ghost
> and these are even as we speak contained
> in three quart jugs

In these lines, Joyce brings together, with strikingly evocative concision, colonial subjugation of land (in China and Ireland) through force and cartography; a suppressive coercion that is closely bound up with human discourse, the 'measured words' 'we speak'. Such subjection involves rejection, of the 'dirt' or debris that refuses to conform to the purifying new order. As Joyce acknowledges, this dimension of the poem draws on the ideas of Mary Douglas, whose *Purity and Danger* atomises the need purity has to reduce that which it spurns to the non-threatening condition of rubbish, whether that be conceptual or human detritus.

Along related lines, a chief preoccupation of the poem is the manner in which lived experiential time is abstracted to clock time, the latter marshalling the former into 'garrisons brief zones / of time and influence':

> until the fixed mesh abstracts
> unerringly each hour
> with all its clamouring brood
> jerking routinely to the tune

Yet the 'clamouring' of reality resists the taxonomic mesh due to its messy particularity, just as one's lifeworld defies total systematisation. Joyce conveys the resistance of dirt, in Douglas's extended sense, to purification through densely punning lines, the ambiguities of which themselves emphasise the fluidity of a supposedly classified, demarcated and regimented world:

> noise of concerns sequestered
> ultimately will get out
> states sundered bleed
> surely each to each
> by breaking bounds ghosts
> traffic through the empty squares

Indeed, the very title word of Joyce's text is ambivalent, trafficking between two senses. Among its meanings, syzygy, in astronomy, can signify either the conjunction or opposition of two heavenly bodies. The strength of this remarkable poem lies in its syzygetic nature; its close correlation of form to a content preoccupied with the opposition that matter, of various kinds, puts up to structuration. (That the word, in prosody, further denotes the admixture of two feet in one metre is also of relevance to the intertwined patterning of the poem's two parts.) In these respects, while *Syzygy* clearly grows out of Joyce's last collection, *stone floods*, it breaks new ground in the compelling intricacy and moving urgency of its formalism.

ALEX DAVIS

A Way for Gay and Lesbian Studies in Ireland?

Eibhear Walshe. *Sex, Nation and Dissent in Irish Writing*. Cork: Cork University Press, 1997. ISBN 1 85918 0132 (hbk) IR£40.00. 1 85918 0140 (pbk) IR£16.95.

Sometimes it might seem as if Irish Studies suffer from a peculiar, yet all the more persistent kind of jet-lag. Throughout the twentieth century the cultural mind in Ireland has been so obsessed with discourses on versions of Irishness that the impact on Ireland of what might be seen as important shifts in Western cultural debates was often significantly delayed. In Ireland the advent of modernism in the aftermath of World War I was put off until the 1960s and the Lemass-era by a period of social and political orthodoxies. Feminism has only left a significant mark in Irish cultural debates since the late eighties, and whether the curtain on postmodernism has yet been lifted in Ireland might be seen in question.

It is a crude story which I have been outlining here and I would not want it to be read too literally. Yet the idea of a cultural jet-lag in Irish Studies gained a certain relevance in my reading of Eibhear Walshe's collection of essays on the homoerotic in Irish writing. Walshe's book is a timely publication – in view of current debates in cultural studies, such a statement could have served well as an opening sentence of this review. Having worked in the fields of both Irish and Gay Studies I was thrilled to see them united for the first time. Yet such a statement at the beginning of my review would implicitly have referred exactly to that kind of narrative about Irish Studies I tried to outline at the beginning; it would have been an academic sigh of relief – *thank God, at last an academic publication on homosexuality in Irish culture* – and an appeal to the current myth of Ireland's coming-of-age as a player in the global league of nations after having overcome the pitfalls of decolonization.

What left me with a feeling of discomfort in reading Walshe's book is that the way it treats its subject of the '*identification* of those Irish writers whose imaginative concerns *centre* around *the* homoerotic and [the] consideration of the ways in which they represent *alternate sexual identities*' (italics are always mine) contributes problematically to such post-national narratives. Eibhear Walshe in his introduction, and many of the authors of the individual essays with him, are very careful in their choice of terminology when talking about same-sex relationships of different kinds. At least since Foucault we know that 'homosexuality' is a historic construct and we have to be careful when representing historic events or persona through our own conceptions. Yet despite this terminological carefulness, the existence of 'unlicensed and divergent sexual identities' is rarely considered a contentious and problematic issue in itself; the book constantly talks about identities, not practices. Consequently, the *identification* of homoerotic intentions or sensibilities in/behind the texts discussed remains the overriding aim of the book. What we are told is that if we read the texts carefully we will either recognise the homoerotic level of meaning underneath the textual surfaces – this counts particularly for the authors from the earlier part of the century – or understand the progressive sexual politics of the more recent and openly gay/lesbian texts.

On a first glance, this is a perfectly feasible common-sense approach to the presently observable marginality of gay and lesbian existence in Irish society. Common sense however is often not indicative of basic truths, but of discursive realities. With its intention of identification, Walshe's present volume is part and parcel of a discourse that constructs 'the contemporary homosexual' by inventing his/her history. The book's most significant faultline concerning such conflicts between essentialist and constructivist views of sexual identity is hidden in the choice of authors and texts. Obviously, choices of inclusion and exclusion are inevitable, yet what I want to argue here is not whether the authors included represent a 'valid' canon of 'homosexual Irish literature'. Of course, other choices could have been made; Desmond Hogan, Colm Toibín and John Broderick spring to mind; a look at the Irish gay and lesbian anthologies published since the law reforms would have been another option. Such other choices, however, would not have made a general difference. What I would really call into question is the range from which the authors and texts are drawn. It is a choice without surprises: Eva Gore Booth, Oscar Wilde, Forrest Reid, Sommerville and Ross, two essays on Elizabeth Bowen, Michael MacLiammoir, Kate O'Brien and Mary Dorcey, Molly Keane, Cathal Ó Searcaigh, David Grant on his own production of *Tangles*, and finally a survey view of gay representation in Irish film. What is notable about this choice is that with the exception of Molly Keane and Neil Jordan (in the film-essay) all authors discussed could be described, however tentatively and problematically, in terms of a 'divergent sexual identity'. What connects Keane and Jordan to this 'community' is that they treat gay and lesbian existence as a 'legitimate subject'. Thus, already the choice of authors constructs the legitimacy of the definite article in the identification of the book's subject of '*the* homoerotic' in Irish literature, while at the same time Walshe's introduction argues that he would not claim 'that such writing constitutes a coherent tradition'. How could it, considering the differences in time and background, and, more importantly, why should it? The definite article, however, implies and constructs an *identity* between these texts which reflects back upon their authors (and implied readers) and is then nicely labelled 'homoerotic'.

Whether *the* homoerotic element in Irish literature is to be found in '*the* homoerotic literature' of Ireland, is, I would argue, a questionable assumption. Such approaches are far from being the radical, subversive criticism they often pose to be. They have their origin in the ideology and politics of early gay and lesbian rights movements. Their aim is to *re*claim either from a 'normalised' heterosexual canon or from the realms of forgotten history what has always been 'ours' by right. As Alan Sinfield argued, what you want to say has more authority if it seems to come through such 'powerful cultural tokens' as for example literary authors. The problem is that such approaches are playing to the tune of dominant discourses. They neatly contain dissident potential within existing power arrangements by neatly organising experience in practicable entities. They tell us what we already 'know': the homosexual is a homosexual is a homosexual. And, surprisingly enough, he/she writes 'homosexual texts' and, more importantly, has always done so one way or other.

A reconstruction of those dynamics which render such questions of homoerotic tradition and identity productive at our current point in history and cultural debate, a cultural archaeology into those subject positions involved in rendering possible the idea of such traditions would have necessitated an inclusion of quite a different range of material. It could, for example, have included the potential for lesbian readings in Bram Stoker's *Dracula*, the fate of Cecilia Cullen in George Moore's *A Drama in Muslin*, the polymorphly perverse paedophile of James Joyce's 'An Encounter' in *Dubliners*, Maurice Leitch's and Dermot Bolger's corrupt homosexual politicians in *The Liberty Lad* and *The Journey Home*, the abuse suffered by John McGahern's protagonist in *The Dark* and Patrick McCabe's *Butcher Boy*, the transgression of sectarian boundaries symbolised by Mal's kissing of Francy in Glenn Patterson's *Burning Your Own*, or Gaye Shortland's hilariously camp rambles through gay Cork in *Mind That 'tis My Brother*. The history of *the* homoerotic in Irish writing is more complex than the myth of liberating authentic gay and lesbian voices makes us believe. Considering common stereotypes of *the* Irish mind, it might come as a surprise, but *the* homoerotic, as my random list of texts should indicate, is not something characteristic of a marginal space of *homoerotic* Irish literature; rather, it is a theme the constitution of which happens right in the centre of what we call Irish literature, and probably contributes more to its definition than has yet been recognised.

But does all this theorising about essentialist and constructivist notions of sexual identity bear any relevance to the actual discussions of individual authors in the individual essays? In his philologically well researched contribution 'Error and Eros: The Fiction of Forrest Reid as a Defence of Homosexuality' Colin Cruise, to choose an example, sets himself the 'task [...] to locate Forrest Reid within a debate on masculinity and sexuality' and contends that 'the novels present an alternative view of the discussion of the nature of homosexuality', linking Reid in his conception of a masculinist aesthetics particularly to Arthur Lyon Raile's *The Wild Rose* and *A Defence of Uranian Love*. The rationale Cruise identifies behind Reid's defence of homosexuality is his urge to harmonise his erotic tendency with the society in which he makes his living by aestheticising a patriarchal culture centred around masculinity. Reid's homosexuality provides a point of origin for Cruise's line of argument: 'Yet there is a less personalised emphasis in his work too, and it is the one I dwell on here, that of the recent history of *men like himself*, men whose sexual inclinations *we call variously "homosexual", "gay" or "queer".' Apostate*, Reid's first volume of autobiography, serves Cruise to authenticate this characterisation of Reid: 'while his apostasy is a rejection of Christianity, its application is towards an alternative sexuality, "the Greek".' Thus Cruise turns the autobiography into his central interpretative tool in explaining Reid's fiction: '*Apostate* is important for providing us with a way into Reid's novels.' Using the autobiography as a presumably authentic point of verification, Cruise comes to recognise the 'real' homoerotic meaning at the centre of the novels, and thus validates his view of Reid's homosexuality, which formed his starting point: 'His Tom Barber trilogy is less about nature and magic and more about the alternatives which they obscure – the natural inclinations of Tom and the hidden history that would vindicate them.' On this basis Cruise challenges 'the idea of Reid as essentially an old-fashioned and untroubling author who purveyed reassuring fictions notable for their idyllic "natural" settings.' His appreciation of Reid as a writer rests solely in his transgression of the social and sexual mores of his time; it is not an appreciation of aesthetic complexities, which to a large extent indeed result from Reid's conscious intention to engage literarily with the experience of male same-sex desire and turn his writing into a fascinating work of art.

Contrary to Cruise, I would view homoeroticism in Reid's writing not as an essential meaning that has to be recovered, but as an end product of a dialogic cultural dynamic that materialises in an intertextual dynamic in his fiction. Rather than being 'a conventional record of the early years of his life' or 'an artistic credo' providing 'a way into Reid's novels', as Cruise reads it, *Apostate* as an autobiographical narrative *text* sits uncomfortably in-between autobiographical *experience* and narrative *fiction*, tentatively working towards creating a connection. 'The primary impulse of the artist springs, I fancy, from discontent,' is its opening sentence and the autobiography literally ends in the silence created by Reid's first confession of love to his friend Andrew Rutherford: 'Then the silence seemed all at once to grow so intense that I felt nothing could ever again break it.' The silence, the literal inability to express an emotional experience due to the absence of a sanctioned signifier in the cultural code of language, is a recurrent problem encountered by Reid's fictional heroes: 'I had nothing to say, or rather I could not say it,' the hero of *Following Darkness* (later reworked as *Peter Waring* in order to bring it into tune with *Apostate*, as Reid explained) has to admit to himself. And, as far as I can see, all of Reid's fictional texts and *Apostate* are intertextually closely linked to each other, be it in the creation of character and events or even actual quotations. Rather than being a poetological meta-text for the novels explaining the aesthetics behind them, *Apostate* forms part of a conscious attempt at textualising experiences without the availability of adequate signifiers. *Apostate* as a text creates a void of silence around which the fictional narratives are centred. While the silence results from the absence of adequate signifiers, the fictional texts exploit such narrative codes and structures which are readily available in Reid's culture: Christianity as an antipode to Greek philosophy and literature as rediscovered in the eighteenth and nineteenth centuries, humanist views of mankind, romanticist ideas of nature, childhood and unity, realist depiction of social and psychological situations, and *fin de siècle* conceptions of art. By being arranged around the central silence, these voices on the one hand create seemingly traditional narratives, yet they also bring these narratives into dialogic relations with each other, eventually filling the central void with a newly constructed meaning, the male subject identified by its male same-sex desire. This dialogue affects a change of perspective within the writing from looking back on insufficient traditional narratives to looking forward into a secure narrative identity which, by implication, facilitates a transgression of the traditional aesthetics. The novels appear no longer as instantiations of specific traditional aesthetic concepts, but rather as making complex and creative use of these without giving final credence to any of them.

Similar or related problems of methodology, I would argue, occur in various other essays of Walshe's collection, though obviously the variety of individual contributors also produces a variety of different perspectives. The question which arises from this situation is whether there is any reason to be found why the first Irish academic book on homoeroticism in Irish writing suffers from this kind of jet-lag, why it restricts itself largely to a theoretical position from the earlier period of gay and lesbian criticism that is, in Thomas Yingling's words, 'content to stop with having established the homosexual content of this or that text or writer' rather than seeing 'homosexuality as the beginning and not the end of a certain literary question'.

The answer to this question may be found in the book's title that is intended to 'operate [. . .] as a set of questions and interrogations into these texts': *Sex, Nation and Dissent.* And indeed, these questions produce answers: 'Irish lesbian and gay writing, in common with most other Irish writing, evinces a connection and a preoccupation with politicised Irish nationalism. [. . .] Quite close to the source of national pride and identity – the creation of an Irish republic – there also existed traces of lesbian and gay writing.' This contention to me epitomises a fundamental gap that opens particularly between the introduction, which presumably outlines the general concepts of the book, and the majority of the individual essays. Quite apart from the point that the introduction never fully explains why an approach to homoeroticism in Irish writing should necessarily be linked to questions of national identity, the essays themselves rather indicate something different: nationality as identity does not play an important part in Irish writing that is concerned with constructing gay or lesbian experiences; and where it does, as in the case of Wilde and MacLiammoir, national identity is ridiculed in an ironic play of self-signification – the Irishman playing English and the Englishman playing Irish. Not surprisingly, Declan Kiberd's essay on Elizabeth Bowen, the only one that particularly centres its attention on aspects of nationality, in the course of its discussion completely looses the sexual theme.

Walshe's strong urge to make a connection between the sexual and the national subject of the literature discussed in his volume provide an explanation why the basic concepts of his collection often fall back on essentialist notions of sexual identity. To Walshe the oppression of sexual difference in twentieth century Ireland is a problem of colonisation: 'The post-colonial struggle to escape the influence of the colonising power became a struggle to escape the gendered relation of male coloniser and to female colonised. Therefore the post-colonial culture could not permit any public, ideological acknowledgement of the actuality of the sexually "other".' Walshe's authority for this position, Kieran Rose's account of the 1993 law reforms in the Republic makes the point even more boldly when he 'puts forward the idea that these changes [i.e. the law reforms] stem from positive traditional Irish values arising from the anti-colonial struggle'. In other words, if the Irish nation suppressed homosexual experiences, it is not her fault; Britain is to blame because Ireland only inherited Britain's homophobia during colonisation. To phrase it rather polemically, Walshe's introduction connects post-colonial and gay/lesbian terminology (terminology, not theory!) to celebrate a particular view of the Irish nation. The real significance of Walshe's book to me seems to lie in its partaking in a reassertion of a reformed and modernised, yet still essentialist nationalism. Walshe's book is one chapter in the story of Modern Ireland as a distinct and strong, yet open minded and liberal European nation. In expressly accepting the homosexual into the national family *Sex, Nation, and Dissent* rewrites the history of the Irish nation, and of Irish nationalism respectively. In approaching such a current and progressive topic as homosexuality Walshe's book casts itself, and with it the Irish intellectual mind, in the light of a modern, multicultural liberalism of Western convention; it goes with the *Zeitgeist* of the Western world and turns the topic of homosexuality into a mere function within those discursive formations of Irish society, with which by now we should be all too well acquainted. The disruptive potential of discourses surrounding homosexuality for debates about the constructedness of national identity is thus effectively contained.

Rather than giving itself to the task of harmonising conceptions of homosexual and Irish national identity, Gay and Lesbian Studies in Ireland harbour a great potential to demonstrate that a wide range of identifications other than national govern the lives of individuals within their societies. Yet this potential of contributing to the deconstruction of monolithic national blocs can only be realised fully if Gay and Lesbian studies remain aware of the historical genesis of *the* modern homosexual and resist the temptation of falling back into the false securities of essentialist sexual politics.

I have chosen to focus my criticism on the book *Sex, Nation and Dissent* rather than the individual essays to highlight some general problems. Therefore I should add at this point that notably those essays in Walshe's collection which engage themselves more fully with current theoretical debates in/about gay and lesbian studies rather than just quoting them as authorities produce the most satisfying readings of their material. I am thinking particularly of Roz Cowman's 'Lost Time. The Smell and Taste of Castle T' on Sommerville and Ross; David Alderson's 'Momentary Pleasures: Wilde and English Virtue'; Patricia Coughlan's 'Women and Desire in the Work of Elizabeth Bowen' and Lance Pettitt's 'Pigs and Provos, Prostitutes and Prejudice. Gay Representation in Irish Film, 1984–1995'. Ironically, Walshe's own essay on Michael MacLiammoir is in many ways quite different from the conceptions outlined in his introduction. For the particular strengths of these individual contributions, the well researched informative detail many of the essays make available, and not at all just because it is the first book on this topic in Irish Studies, *Sex, Nation and Dissent* surely achieves one of its aims despite all its problems: 'to open up a context for further research'. In this context Walshe's book will become, I am sure, a standard point of reference for future work to be done in this field.

KLAUS GUNNAR SCHNEIDER

High-minded Interventions

Joseph Morrison Skelly. *Irish Diplomacy at the United Nations 1945–1965: National Interests and the International Order*. Dublin: Irish Academic Press, 1997. ISBN 0 7165 2574 7. IR£32.00

As an American diplomat dealing with the United Nations over some eight years in Vienna and then in Geneva, I became aware, early on, that Ireland played a role in our deliberations weightier than her size would seem to warrant. The opinions of Irish diplomats were regularly deferred to and, standardly, Irish diplomats were sought out for leadership positions. This new book goes a long way towards explaining this phenomenon.

Mary Robinson, while President, supplied a remarkably sensible foreword, describing this book as 'thorough, well researched and documented, and a welcome addition to the study of Irish diplomacy'. It is, indeed, all that and even more – it is that rarity of historical scholarship: a thesis-driven work in which the analysis is smoothly integrated into compellingly-readable narrative history. At the beginning, the author states that his investigation will rely on 'national interests as the primary conceptual apparatus for interpreting Irish diplomacy at the UN'. This is as welcome as it is realistic. Too regularly, as Skelly frequently notes, Irish foreign policy is presented as above it all, placed, particularly by politicians, on an altruistic plane fit only for a people fed on fantasies of their unique moral stature' (an observation cited from Joe Lee). However, as I will argue, Skelly is himself not entirely free of this compulsion to gloss Irish interventions in a high-minded light.

Despite the book's title, the actual period covered is 1956–65, the first decade of Ireland's membership of the United Nations, Ireland having been finally voted in in a package deal (December 1955) The narration is, for the most part, organised chronologically by successive general assemblies. Separate consideration is given to the nuclear non-proliferation initiative and to peacekeeping in the Congo. On the central issue of Ireland's guiding posture in the UN at that tune, Skelly identifies two opposing views which, throughout this decade, jostled for pre-eminence in Iveagh House. While both views sprang from the realistic recognition that Ireland, as a small country, needed to rely upon international law and the moral force of the UN, they differed in their normative interpretations of how to apply this in a world dominated by power realities. The first view was pro-Western; the other Skelly simply terms 'independent'. While this seems an apt term insofar as it reflects Ireland's determination not to be viewed as an automatic member of a voting-bloc, a caustic observer could suggest less positive terms for some of its more quixotic manifestations.

The pro-Western view held sway as Ireland entered the UN. Liam Cosgrave, as foreign minister, laid out to the Dáil the three principles which would guide the country as it embarked on its first general assembly (the Eleventh, beginning in the autumn of 1956): unequivocal adherence to the UN Charter, a position of independence in which issues would be judged on their merits, and support for defence of the free world against the spread of Communism. Skelly notes that scholars have dentified an 'inherent tension' between the second and third principles, a judgment which he shares. By doing so, he betrays his own intellectual bias. Throughout, he treats being anti-Communist as somehow risible, certainly not altogether respectable (he cites apparently approvingly, for instance, Krishna Menon's dismissive reference to 'the anti-communist bug'), and he posits a moral equivalency between the democratic nations and those of the Soviet-bloc. This attitude of treating, in a value-free fashion, Communism as though it were a legitimate political system like any other – the prevailing posture among Western intelligentsia since the 1960s – was always without intellectual merit and is now, with the wholesale collapse of Communism in Europe, simply tiresome. Indeed, it's precisely the sort of judgmental bias which gives rise to gibes about academics in ivory towers where theory is preferred to real-world consequences. Unfortunately, Skelly allows this misguided moral relativism anachronistically to infect his judgments of events and policy positions taken in what was not a simpler but rather a clearer-thinking age.

Certainly, Cosgrave perceived no inconsistency in his principles – in his eyes, to decide, independently, on an issue upon its merits was to do so on the basis of democracy and human rights, precisely that is, upon the principles embedded by the West in the UN Charter. Characteristic is Skelly's dismissal of American diplomatic efforts over the Hungarian crisis of 1956 as driven by 'the Cold War nature of this issue'. One would have thought that the crushing of this nationalist revolt by Soviet tanks vital to the interests of any democratic nation. Irish UN Ambassador Fred Boland certainly saw it in this light, arguing that the issues were not Cold War issues but matters of right and wrong. (Surely, this is also the first time that granting Cardinal Mindszenty refuge in the American embassy in Budapest has been described, as Skelly does, as 'protective custody'.)

Skelly treats the lack of real action by the UN in this crisis as a paradigm for continuing great power, specifically US, use of the UN. In his judgment, the great powers, determining that intervention in a given crisis would be too risky, allow the UN to shoulder the blame 'until the odds of success on the ground' improve. He cites, *inter alia*, Bosnia as a 1990s example. This is a judgment regularly made by Irish commentators. Garret FitzGerald actually laid the blame for years of brutal Serbian use of force on the US.[1] His argument was that, 'several years' back, a peace agreement had been reached between the warring parties but the Clinton administration encouraged the Bosnian government to 'toughen its stand', resulting in renewed Serbian aggression. In truth, anyone who believes that the Serbs ever intended to adhere to any of the multitude of agreements, truces, or ceasefires that were brokered is operating from the planet of wishful thinking. The only way to stop Serbian aggression was to confront it militarily, and this could only be done successfully after the Croatian and Bosnian governments created armed and trained armies capable of doing so. More pointedly, these 'odds of success on the ground' didn't just happen – it was covert American assistance which enabled the Croats and Bosnian Muslims to create their armies which defeated the Serbians on the ground and it was this which compelled the Serbians to lift their siege of Sarajevo and grudgingly observe the Dayton accords. Dr FitzGerald remarks, 'foreign policy founded on righteous indignation, that takes insufficient account of realities on the ground, ends up doing more harm than good'. The cognitive dissonance exemplified in this remark has had a long history in Irish diplomacy at the political level. It also marked, as we shall now see, the second phase of Ireland's first decade in the UN.

In 1957, de Valera returned to power, Frank Aiken became foreign minister, and the Irish posture at the UN shifted into, in Skelly's term, an 'independent' phase. Skelly argues strongly – against what he terms the 'misinterpretations' of previous scholars – that it was de Valera's 'predilections' which defined this period. He makes a persuasive case for, at least, de Valera's watchful and approving oversight. Nevertheless, it seems clear that the motive force for this shift in Ireland's UN posture was, indeed, Aiken's hardheaded determination to stand out in the UN, with Conor Cruise O'Brien, as the counsellor for UN affairs in Iveagh House, supplying the intellectual back-up. Skelly additionally describes their new posture as 'activist'. It might perhaps be more accurately described as playing the 'gadfly'.

The most famous instance of Aiken's 'activist and independent' stance was his changing of Ireland's vote, in opposition to the US's position, to one of support for inscribing on the general assembly's agenda the question of Red China's admission to the UN. Skelly accepts Aiken's contention that Secretary of State Dulles, instead of approaching Aiken himself over this dispute, asked Cardinal Spellman to intervene. He describes this as 'ham-fisted'. However, in presenting this version of the American response, Skelly does not use primary sources but relies, rather, on Dermot Keogh's *Twentieth-Century Ireland*. Unfortunately (for Skelly's argument, that is), Keogh, who does, here, use primary sources (and on the American side they have long been open) cites *no* evidence for any contact whatsoever between American officials and Cardinal Spellman, and he notes as well that the American ambassador in Dublin – who had previously served as a senior State Department official – did not believe that any such approach had been made to the cardinal[2] (a point Skelly does not mention). It would seem far likelier, then, that this contention is a product of Aiken's imagination, determined on a demeaning American spin. Skelly notes, after all, that the change in the Irish vote provoked a general outcry among both American and Irish Catholics (Bishop Browne of Galway particularly excoriating the move), and he cites, as well, the origin of Aiken's 'anti-Americanism' in his failed attempt, in 1941, to bully FDR into supplying Ireland with the armaments needed to maintain neutrality against the British. What we see at work in Aiken's creation of this story – which has reached folklore status – is an early working of a phenomenon which had reached epidemic levels in Ireland by the 1980s: myth-making about the motivations of US foreign policy by maliciously personalising its formulation. Hearings on American policy towards Cuba in the Oireachtas foreign affairs committee, for example, would never consider the brutal realities of Castro's police-state – no, such hearings, as well as press commentary, would simply condemn American policy as 'immoral, illegal, and bullying' and put it all down to the president's desire to secure Cuban American votes in Florida. This is not a reasoned perception of foreign policy.

A second instance of Aiken's posturing on cost-free issues was his proposal for mutual troop withdrawal in Central Europe. What possible real-world experience could he (or O'Brien) have brought to this critically tense issue? Indeed, when confronted by NATO ambassadors in Dublin, de Valera admitted that he had no intimate knowledge of the military situation. All in all, an apt illustration of the downside of having inexperienced politicians meddling in diplomacy. (Ambassador Boland opposed both the shift in the China vote and the troop withdrawal proposal.) Indeed, as we have already noted, it has been an occasional characteristic of Irish foreign policy at the political level to wilfully disregard unpleasant realities and engage in wishful thinking or even Pollyanish hyperbole. The current foreign minister, for instance, was reported as declaring, on signing the land-mine ban treaty, that these were 'lethal devices which serve no military purpose' – an observation which would certainly be news to any infantry commander facing, across an armistice line, an enemy force vastly outnumbering his own and under the command of a paranoid and wholly unpredictable dictator. But, then, these are real-world considerations.

Skelly notes a number of other instances of Aiken's 'unrealistic streak'. Here must be included his Areas of Law proposal – to the political field what his troop withdrawal idea was to the military. However, in an altogether different category would be his interventions on decolonisation in general and on the specific subject of the non-proliferation of nuclear weapons. On Algeria, he rejected the specious French argument that Algeria constituted an integral part of France and he urged negotiation on the basis of self-determination – then a highly controversial view but one which matched that taken by then Senator John F. Kennedy. On the Middle East, his proposal for principles underlying a comprehensive peace would, if they had been delivered as Aiken originally had them, have marked out for Ireland a truly moral and enlightened stance. On Tibet, he worked closely with the US on a resolution condemning Chinese violations of human rights in that sad land.

This close cooperation with the US once again became the norm in the latter years of Aiken's involvement with the UN (in 1959 Seán Lemass had become taoiseach[3] and in 1961 Conor Cruise O'Brien left the Irish delegation, seconded to the UN secretariat). Irish support for the US was particularly marked throughout the Cuban missile crisis. (I must correct Skelly here – it was not a 'blockade' but a 'quarantine' which JFK imposed, a difference bearing vital distinctions in international law.) The great accomplishment of Aiken in this period, though, was the 1961 resolution on nuclear non-proliferation. Throughout, Aiken displayed both persistence and a willingness to take on board the legitimate concerns of the US and others. In recognition, when the Non-Proliferation Treaty was signed in 1968, he was invited to be its first signatory. Skelly concludes his book, fittingly, with a chapter on Ireland's courageous decision to accede to the Secretary General's request for troops to protect peace in the Congo.

I would make one suggestion to the author: the 1960s are past and the attitudes then trendy are now passé. Specifically, the revisionist interpretation of American Cold War diplomacy – which was always derived from a shabby abuse, or even disregard, of historical sources – is no longer taken seriously, not even in mainstream academia (it was never taken seriously by those who actually formulate US foreign policy). I am all too aware, of course, that this insidious virus did not reach potency in Ireland until the late-1970s and, hence, still exerts a residual influence – which is all the more cause for an Irish diplomatic historian to be on guard against its devious mix of myth-making and misinformation. No serious historian today, for instance, would still contend that American policy in Central America was one of support for right-wing governments repressive of their peoples. Rather, as we claimed then, our policy was one of restraining repression, whether from the right or from the left, and nurturing democracy. The means we sometimes employed were tortuous, but not incommensurate with the tortured history of most of the countries of the region. Democracy, after all, has seldom been more than an aspiration in Latin American political culture, and inequalities are deeply embedded. To cite a recent case-in-point, President Aristide was one of those who used to take his lead from those who would distort American intentions and attack American 'imperialism' – his mentors being those leftist intellectuals whose 1960s-style radicalism remained not just unreconstructed by reality but driven by a sort of cognitive degeneration fueled by intellectual petulance. But Aristide learned first-hand the intent and benefits of the US's benevolent hegemony and, like other regional leaders such as Oscar Arias and the late José Napoleón Duarte, he was grateful both publicly and privately.

The truth is that today the nations of the Western Hemisphere are united in their determination that the establishment and continuance of democratic governments in each of the countries of the region is the legitimate concern of all the countries of the region. Today, the only dictatorship left in Latin America is Castro's Cuba; a salutary object-lesson for those who would carp at America's dedication to democracy at home and abroad (a real-world constant sometimes lost sight of by Skelly).

Nevertheless, this book is the way to write diplomatic history, particularly that involving a multilateral institution such as the UN. I say this, despite my occasional misgivings regarding Skelly's interpretations, for you cannot begin to understand the 'why', until you know who did what and when, and this study is a model of a detailed examination proceeding from internal discussions, with named participants and memo-drafters, to final resolution, taking in corridor conversations and telephone calls along the way. Throughout, Skelly's understanding of UN diplomatic mores and procedures comes across as authentic. His description, for instance, of Aiken's 'explanation of vote' on China would be illuminating for those still condemnatory of the US vote to seat the Democratic Coalition as representing Cambodia. I would suggest, though, that in assessing US intentions – in a study so concerned throughout with US policies and actions – that he ought to have made some use of US sources and not have relied so wholly on Irish accounts of conversations and exchanges. For instance, his description of American bargaining tactics – amounting, in his terms, to 'cajoling' and 'arm-twisting' – relies solely on claims by Conor Cruise O'Brien, hardly a disinterested or unbiased observer (later, Skelly dismisses similar strictures directed by O'Brien at Irish diplomacy as 'exaggerated and inaccurate').[4]

Well, we must all acknowledge our own inclinations to bias and I would not want anything I have written here to be seen to detract from the high regard in which the abilities of professional Irish diplomats are wont to be held or from the genuine contributions which Irish diplomacy has made to the betterment of the world order. In his introduction, Skelly claims that his book will chronicle an 'Irish success story'. Indeed, it has done so.

Notes and References

1 US foreign policy to benefit from Clinton's second term', *The Irish Times*, 9 November 1966.

2 Dermot Keogh, *Twentieth-Century Ireland: Nation and State* (Dublin, 1994), pp. 235-7.

3 Again, Skelly argues, persuasively, that Lemass, as Taoiseach, had a determining role in the Irish posture at the UN; this runs counter to the traditional view that Lemass was content to allow Aiken a free hand at the UN, for which see John Horgan *Seán Lemass: the Enigmatic Patriot* (Dublin, 1997), pp. 193-4.

4 I must also note that these critical judgments directed at Irish diplomacy in the UN by O'Brien some years after he had left the diplomatic service were part-and-parcel of the wilfully biased and even occasionally mean-spirited slurs he has made a career of directing at US foreign policy. See, for instance, his characterisation of President Clinton's policy towards Haiti as hypocritical and wholly driven by domestic political concerns; *On the Eve of the Millennium* (New York, 1995), pp. 89-90 and 135-6.

GEORGE T. DEMPSEY

The Puritan Generation

J. Anthony Gaughan (ed.). *Memoirs of Senator Joseph Connolly, a founder of modern Ireland.* Dublin: Irish Academic Press, 1996. ISBN 0 1765 2611 5, pp481, hbk IR£35.

Few public figures from the first decades of the Irish State produced memoirs, and accounts of the War of Independence and Civil War often focus on those years to the exclusion of earlier formative experiences; all the more reason to thank F.X. Martin for persuading Joseph Connolly (1885–1961) to write his memoirs. Fr Gaughan has now edited and published them.

Connolly was the son of a Belfast master baker. He was apprenticed to an engineering firm, which he left after experiencing various forms of exploitation and petty tyranny, and finally to a Protestant furniture-maker; he set up his own business in April 1915. His descriptions of poverty and exploitation witnessed in Edwardian Belfast help to explain his simplistic attribution of Ulster Unionism to elite manipulation. He combined friendly relations with individual Unionists with inability to take their views seriously and overestimation of the residual Protestant Liberal tradition.

Connolly was active in Sinn Féin and the Ulster Literary Theatre. He deeply respected Griffith; readers of Griffith's journalism will recognise his influence on Connolly. He served in the Belfast Irish Volunteers and carried MacNeill's counteranding order north. (Connolly married Roisin McGavock, MacNeill's niece. He loved her and consulted her before major decisions, but since he is describing his public life he says little about her – a natural reticence, however disappointing. They had eight children; five entered religious life.) Connolly was arrested and imprisoned after the Easter Rising and spent some time in prison; in the 1918 election he contested Mid-Antrim for Sinn Féin. He gives a vivid account of Belfast during the War of Independence (incidentally mentioning the use of bin-lids to raise the alarm in nationalist districts) and the difficulties of business life during the postwar boom and depression (compounded by the Belfast Boycott, which he actively supported though it damaged his own business). He describes the narcissistic multiple turncoat Herbert Pim and the nationalist Presbyterian Minister J.A.H. Irwin.

During the Truce Connolly was sent New York as Consul; he could get no-one to manage his business and had to close it at a sizable loss (which the Connollys accepted as a lesser sacrifice than others had made; only incidentally are we told Roisin was pregnant). His family later moved to Dublin. Connolly opposed the Treaty, but believed Republicans should have remained in the Dáil as a constitutional opposition. He was outraged by the executions of Childers and other Republican leaders, resigned as Consul and returned to Ireland to help re-organise Sinn Féin after the Civil War. For some years he exported Irish goods to America (he comments scathingly on the shortcomings of Irish manufacturers).

From 1928 Connolly led Fianna Fail in the Senate. In the 1932 de Valera government he became Minister for Posts and Telegraphs. (He turned down the Ministry of Education because he could not speak Irish fluently.) Connolly also represented Ireland at the League of Nations (which he thought ineffective) and went on diplomatic missions. In 1933 Connolly became Minister for Lands, and focused on speeding up land division. When the Senate was abolished in 1936 Connolly joined the Civil Service heading the Board of Works until 1950. He was Controller of Censorship during the war; his smug account contrasts with Ó Drisceoil's *Censorship in Ireland 1939–45*, which portrays censors as petty bullies equating government and state.

Connolly shared the traditional nationalist belief in a nation of smallholders supported by highly decentralised industries, and thought Lemass focused too much on the bigger towns and fly-by-night foreign industrialists. He feared emigration and rural depopulation were continuing the work of nineteenth-century landlordism. His friendship with de Valera broke down in 1945 over this. A brief paragraph about de Valera's hostility to criticism and fondness for yes-men cost Connolly more pain than anything else in the memoir. (This was physical pain; Connolly was dying of heart disease.) He hoped the new generation would revive the ideals of his youth.

It is easy to criticise Connolly. He combined adminstrative capability with wildly unrealistic political beliefs. He lived in Dublin and Belfast yet idealised the small farmer. He disliked debate and distrusted coalitions and minority governments as handicapping principled leadership. The ideas that compromise might be desirable, that majority governments are less accountable, and that the opposition might deserve input into policy are never mentioned.

Connolly shared the puritanism of his generation; he was a teetotaller, disliked risqué plays, and saw the post-1940 *Irish Press* as excessively sensationalist. He disapproved of Irish government departments having large headquarters as unbefitting a small country. He distrusted hire purchase and the stock market. He was not anti-semitic (he records admiration for an old Belfast Jew and intervened on behalf of a German Jewish art historian) but his comment that, before Buchenwald and Dachau, the case of Kevin Barry showed how prisoners of war could be mistreated, suggests failure of imagination. Connolly says Protestants should be thankful to keep Christ Church and St Patrick's, and speaks of the conversion of Dublin Castle chapel from Anglican to Catholic worship as redeeming part of Ireland from foreign conquerors.

This puritanism also produced a social conscience (he admired Franklin D. Roosevelt and complained MacCarthyites retrospectively denounced radical views which were justifiable responses to the Depression), and concern for honesty in business and public life. Connolly refused to make upholstered furniture which hid shoddy workmanship; he resisted political favouritism in the civil service. His sacrifices for self-determination were not the fetishism of sacrifice which warped many Republicans. Connolly describes his bank manager in 1916 advising him to give creditors ten shillings in the pound, though he could pay more. Connolly said this was contrary to Catholic and Sinn Féin principles; he would sooner lose everything than cheat them.

Connolly's worldview may be criticised, but not despised. These memoirs should be supplemented by a comprehensive biography of a man who did the state some service.

PATRICK MAUME

Reconfiguring History

Margaret Ward. *Hannah Sheehy Skeffington: A Life*. Cork: Attic Press, 1997. ISBN 1 85594 179 1. IR£45.00 hbk. ISBN 1 85594 187 2. IR£14.95 pbk.

Anthony Bradley and Maryann Gialanella Valiulis (eds.). *Gender and Sexuality in Modern Ireland*. Amherst: University of Massachusetts, 1997. ISBN 1 558490131 7.

Maryann Gialanella Valiulis and Mary O'Dowd (eds.). *Women & Irish History: Essays in honour of Margaret MacCurtain*. Dublin: Wolfhound Press, 1997. ISBN 0-86327-579-6.

The titles under review here all interrelate in a satisfying manner. Two share an editor; Margaret MacCurtain is a contributor to one collection of essays, the other is a *festschrift* in her honour which acknowledges her importance as pioneer of the academic study of Irish women's history. Several authors have essays in each collection and the author of the biography has contributed to one of the collections. There are essays which enhance our understanding of events discussed in the biography notably by the introduction of comparison with contemporary happenings in Europe and the United States, an exercise which questions theories of Irish exceptionalism.

Details of the life of Hanna Sheehy Skeffington, feminist, suffragette, pacifist and Sinn Féin activist are well known from previous biographies, studies of the suffrage movement and from Margaret Ward's own *Unmanageable Revolutionaries*. Member of a nationalist political family, founder of the Irishwomen's Franchise League and of the *Irish Citizen*, the journal of radical feminism, Hanna is an iconic figure of the Irish women's movement. She emerges from this work as an attractive personality, gifted intellectually, with a great capacity for friendship, a strong sense of fun and compelling powers of oratory. Margaret Ward's account of her early life provides an interesting glimpse of Catholic, nationalist, middle-class life in Dublin in the late nineteenth and early twentieth centuries. The first half of this biography which describes her marriage to Frank Skeffington, her espousal of rationalism and corresponding rejection of religion, her growing feminist activism, is a lively and engrossing read. The description of Hanna's visits to the GPO and the Royal College of Surgeons with supplies of food at the start of the 1916 Rising conveys the sense of adventure in the early days of the undertaking: 'The rebels had great fun unpacking the parcels and hearing who had contributed the various tins of soup, ham and salmon.' The account of Frank's unprovoked murder by a British army officer is powerful and convincingly explains Hanna's conversion to republican activism.

The second part of the biography highlights this activism and seems to me less compelling. Hanna's life epitomised the conflict between Irish nationalism and feminism. Prior to 1916, she had argued strongly against Inighnidhe na hÉireann's and Cumann na mBan's prioritising of nationalist over feminist causes. The murder of her husband and her subsequent treatment by British authorities resulted in her significant involvement in Sinn Féin and in cooperation between Cumann na mBan and suffragists. After independence, when bitterly opposed to the Free State, Hanna felt that the priority was to rebuild the radical republicanism of Connolly whom she greatly admired. Margaret Ward writes that she believed if the Republic were achieved the 'Irish State would be reconstituted. It would no longer be anti-woman and anti-working class, favouring the rich and well-connected.' This seems at odds with Hanna's earlier insights into the conservative nature of Irish nationalism, particularly when one considers that she 'was forthright in regretting the continued refusal of Sinn Féin to admit Cumann na mBan . . . as a right to its conventions.' The treatment of Hanna's activities in the 1920s would have benefited from a more critical analysis. A case in point was her participation in the Cumann na mBan protest at O'Casey's *The Plough and the Stars*. Although Margaret Ward's account of this episode pinpoints the irony of Hanna's objection to O'Casey's depiction of 'looting as a device to demonstrate how far removed from those who planned the Rising were the destitute members of the Dublin working class' (Frank had lost his life as a result of his efforts to prevent looting), she does not comment on Hanna's choice of Mrs Pearse, 'that valiant woman who gave both her sons for freedom' as typifying the women of Easter Week. One would surely have expected a feminist to choose an active participant in the Rising as exemplifying the women of 1916, rather than someone, however worthy, whose involvement was based solely on her relationship to male participants.

Margaret Ward cites Hanna's participation in local government as refutation of the charge that she was engaged in merely 'opposing the government in the 1920s'. She served on Dublin Corporation from 1920 to 1924 and was elected to Dublin County Council in 1925. A fuller discussion in the biography of her work as councillor would have been useful (we are merely told she was elected to Dublin County Council), both to reiterate this point, and to further explore the extent of her social and feminist concerns. Incidentally, the first woman to be elected to Dublin Corporation, Sarah Cecilia Harrison, is described, and given separate index entries, as both Sarah Harrison and Cecilia Harrison.

Sadly Hanna's attempt in the 1940s, to get elected to the Dáil as a member of the Women's Social and Progressive League resulted in the loss of her deposit, an illustration of how activist women were marginalised for decades after the abstentionist policy of 1922. She remained an energetic and committed campaigner for equality until her death in 1946. One cannot help regretting that her principles forbade her playing a part within the political establishment. Margaret Ward thinks that had she compromised and achieved a place in government her feminist voice would have been stifled. Perhaps, but is it not possible that with her powers of intellect and oratory she might have managed to introduce a feminist voice into government?

Some themes are mentioned tantalisingly but not developed. Hanna resolutely avoided housework and, despite straitened circumstances, employed a maid and, on the birth of her son, a nursemaid. This 'refusal to become immersed in domesticity' is seen by the biographer as an assertion of personal independence, possible because of the existence of a vast pool of cheap female labour. Was Hanna unconscious of this irony? Did she allow that one could be housewife and feminist? When the Irish Housewives' Association, a feminist organisation was founded, with her approval, she objected to the name remarking that members 'were not married to the house'. Hilda Tweedy, founder of the IHA, explained that the term 'housewife' was used in the name of the association to defy critics who jeered at them for being housewives. Usefully Catríona Clear's 'No Feminine Mystique', in *Women and Irish History* explores attitudes to women and housework. Her examination of popular literature aimed at women reveals that advice proffered to the housewife suggested 'precious little idealization of the home-maker's lot'. The best-selling *Women's Life*, an 'interesting and attractive' Irish women's magazine of the 1930s and '40s, would appear to have offered role models, other than happy home-makers to its readers. It carried lengthy interviews with working women who were depicted as strong and independent and 'professed not to be waiting around for marriage'. The magazine headlined achievements of women in the arts, culture, politics and sport. Catríona Clear's work explores the complexity of the perception of women's position in Irish society; despite the enshrinement of woman as home-maker in the 1937 constitution, 'there was in certain quarters an attitude of hostility and ridicule towards both representatives and representations of women in charge of households'. Did these 'quarters' include contemporary feminists?

Rosemary Cullen Owens's essay on pacifism in *Women and Irish History* demonstrates the deep 'cleavage' in the Irish International League in the 1920s resulting from differences between women of the 'really pacifist group' and those, including Hanna Sheehy Skeffington, who would put 'freedom before peace'. A delegate at the 1926 Women's International League for Peace and Freedom congress deplored the 'intense nationalist propaganda' of some Irish speakers. The demise of the international women's peace movement in Ireland was caused by the conviction of some of its members that the 'struggle for national independence was not complete'. Margaret Ward again covers this territory in an essay in *Gender and Sexuality in Modern Ireland* where she provides evidence that contrary to belief, Hanna Sheehy Skeffington 'was not a pacifist when it came to a consideration of the Irish situation . . . completely independent of any traumatic reaction to Frank Sheehy Skeffington's murder'. Hanna wrote that if there was any hope of a 'swift uprising' freeing Ireland from British rule then she 'would consider Irishmen justified resorting to arms'. She went on to say that she held 'no such hopes' and felt that 'freedom for small nations lies in Justice by Arbitration'. One could argue that here Hanna is citing a hypothetical situation which she felt was unlikely to happen, nonetheless, I think Margaret Ward is right in that this extract reveals that Hanna Sheehy Skeffington's pacifism was not all-embracing even before the Rising.

Women and Irish History is a collection which provides rich accounts of the lives of ordinary women and their status in society including Elizabeth Steiner-Scott's 'To Bounce a Boot Off Her Now & Then . . .' an account, sourced from late nineteenth century newspapers and the Criminal Index Files, of wife-beating in Ireland. The inability of abused women to support themselves and their children frequently compelled them to appeal against their husbands' custodial sentences. It appears that the perceived decline in the practice in England towards the end of the century was not replicated here, nor was reforming legislation which increased the matrimonial jurisdiction of the Magistrates' Courts, extended to Ireland. In the writer's opinion, the lack of outcry at the extraordinary number of wife-beating cases reported in the Irish press suggests that it was regarded merely as petty crime, a perception reiterated by a remark of Hanna Sheehy Skeffington quoted in the Ward biography 'that a wife beater had received a lighter sentence' than the two months imposed on her for window-breaking.

Mary E. Daly's 'Turn on the Tap', shows that as late as 1971 over 42 per cent of rural homes had no running water, a reflection, perhaps, of the low status of many rural women. The most vocal opponent of the government's 1960s campaign to spread 'the gospel of piped water' was the National Farmers' Association who felt that the scheme would increase local authority rates and not benefit members with their own water supply. The government enlisted the aid of the Irish Countrywomen's Association in the campaign which meant a clash between male and female rural organisations and, presumably, between some husbands and wives. Interestingly in her recent biography of Muriel Gahan, Geraldine Mitchell describes this episode as government support for the ICA campaign, rather than the other way round. She quotes *The Irish Times*: 'It is quite a triumph for the ICA . . . such speed in getting government support can seldom have been achieved by any association.' However, despite the ICA's efforts, Mary Daly concludes that NFA opposition delayed the availability of water to many rural women and condemned them to the drudgery of drawing water into the last third of this century.

Gender and Sexuality in Modern Ireland is an eclectic collection of essays which laudably attempts to cross the 'national narratives with counternarratives' of gender and sexuality. Themes range from the poetry of Ní Chuilleanáin, McGuckian and Kinsella, to the 'outing' of Roger Casement. In her challenging 'The Posthumous life of Roger Casement,' Lucy McDiarmuid suggests an acceptance of Casement's homosexuality, as well as his patriotism, in 1990s Ireland. The Irish denial of Casement's homosexuality for decades is perhaps symbolic of an attitude that only 'real men' could die for Ireland. In 'Queering the Irish Renaissance' Adrian Frazier discusses Edward Martyn, George Moore and W.B. Yeats in the context of their 'uncategorical masculinities' and explores the unease engendered by aesthetes in the cultural nationalist movement. These essays are welcome portents of an increasing interest in the exploration of gay identities in Irish history and literature.

There is also much useful material here for those interested in women's history. Maureen Murphy in 'The Fionnuala Factor' shows that for many young women emigration to the United States represented opportunity rather than suffering exile. Many returned with increased self-esteem and self-confidence, in control of their lives, having earned their own dowries. Those who stayed away enabled siblings to join them and became as it were, heads of the family in exile. There is a serendipity, for the purpose of this review, in the inclusion of an essay, 'Godly Burden' by Margaret MacCurtain which surveys Catholic sisterhood in Ireland in this century.

Nuns, despite their image as docile and submissive figures in medieval headdresses, were vital figures in the provision of health services and education. The status of lay sisters, who entered the convent without a dowry and who looked after traditional women's tasks within the convent is discussed critically here. They had no vote in community affairs nor were they eligible to stand for election as superior. Their inferior status reflected the divisions in Irish society and indeed suggests an analogy with the position of women in the world outside the convent. Recent troubling revelations on the running of orphanages and Magdalene asylums in Ireland in this century suggest the need for further scholarly work in this field.

In 'Women and Fiction', Virginia Woolf discussed the absence of a record of the lives of women. History, she said 'is the history of the male line, not of the female'. Thankfully, as the works reviewed here reveal, some records of women's lives have since been written into history. There is still much to be done. The challenge is not only to recover the lives of women in the past but also, in Linda Colley's words 'to reconfigure the . . . history of nationalism, empire, frontiers, and political authority – so that women and issues to do with them can be brought properly into the story'. The task of retrieving archival material pertaining to the history of Irishwomen has lately received government recognition and funding. The resulting Women's History Project, under the directorship of Dr Maria Luddy, is at present uncovering and surveying sources relevant to the history of women in Ireland with a view to producing a directory and database. Reports of the project to date suggest the discovery of rich new sources which will enhance research and scholarship.

CARMEL FARRELLY

Reading the North

Thomas Hennessey. *A History of Northern Ireland 1920–1996*. Dublin: Gill and Macmillan, 1997. ISBN 0 7171 2623 4. IR£40.00 hbk. ISBN 0 7171 2400 2. IR£12.99 pbk.

Feargal Cochrane. *Unionist Politics and the Politics of Unionism since the Anglo-Irish Agreement*. Cork: Cork University Press, 1997. ISBN 1 85918 138 4. IR£40.00 hbk. ISBN 1 85918 139 2 IR£17.95 pbk.

Henry Patterson. *The Politics of Illusion: A Political History of the IRA*. London: Serif, 1997. ISBN 1 897959 31 1. STG£14.99.

John Darby. *Scorpions in a Bottle: Conflicting Cultures in Northern Ireland*. London: Minority Rights Group, 1997. ISBN 1 873194 16 1. STG£11.95.

Books dealing with the Northern Irish conflict are produced in vast numbers. Who reads them? Not, for the most part, the protagonists of the conflict nor, sadly, very many university students. Many in each group tend, like Lady Bracknell, not to approve of anything that tampers with natural ignorance. But many in each group could certainly gain something from Thomas Hennessey's valuable new history of Northern Ireland. It is not simply a book about the conflict, although it would have been much less likely to exist without it. Indeed, violence pervades its three hundred pages of text: 'The birth of Northern Ireland was a bloody one', we are reminded early on; and the book ends with Sinn Féin and the wider Republican movement, and a consideration of the possibility of their entering a more conventional political realm than that which made them famous. Between these two passages, Dr Hennessey draws on some good archival and newspaper material and he presents a fair-minded narrative of Northern Irish history. Single-volume accounts of Northern Ireland's past can be very useful, particularly for a general readership, and this one deserves to be read.

Hennessey is unafraid to reveal the deeply sectarian quality of Northern Irish society, which is nicely and repeatedly demonstrated in the book. The period between 1928 and 1962 he is happy to call a cold war. Everyone (unless they live in a sensory deprivation tank) recognizes the fundamentally divided nature of Northern Ireland during the post-1960s troubles; but Hennessey is lucid in stressing that earlier periods of the region's history exhibited the same division. 'What the evidence . . . suggests is that many of the old fears, myths and prejudices that Protestants and Catholics held of each other at the state's formation survived well into the second half of the twentieth century.' The author points out that unionist claims that they distinguished between political and religious Catholics in fact did little to help community relations. To little avail did Basil Brooke declare in 1935 that unionists 'had no quarrel with Roman Catholics as such, but with their members who strive to tear them from the Empire. It was a political and not a religious quarrel.'

The context for unionist actions has partly been defined, during much of Northern Ireland's history, by the sense of siege which they have experienced. Enemies within and without threatened their state. Thus they lacked the confidence necessary to facilitate magnanimity; and their lack of magnanimity helped to deepen the conditions in which they felt besieged. Nationalist actions do help explain (if not necessarily justify) unionist behaviour. As Hennessey observes, the Gaelicization of southern Ireland, together with the use of aggressive definitions and methods by Irish Republicans, led to unionists being less prepared to identify themselves as Irish. Nationalist actions and attitudes also led unionists to feel permanently surrounded and infiltrated by their historic opponents. Such was the political context within which Northern Ireland's famous discrimination occurred. Hennessey is clear that discrimination did unquestionably take place. But he is also shrewd enough to note that it was less extensive than is frequently suggested, and that it was by no means a practice exclusive to unionists.

Many who pick up this book will do so in order to understand why *current* politics is as it is in Northern Ireland. What has Hennessey to say which sheds light here? First, he shows that 1990s British governmental approaches have, in a sense, deep roots: as early as 1972 London suggested that Northern Ireland would remain in the United Kingdom as long as its majority so wished, but simultaneously looked for an Irish dimension with relation to the Republic of Ireland. Second, he notes that the 1970s Sunningdale Agreement, which some observers have seen as a kind of pre-echo of the proposed 1990s political deal, was flawed in that those involved in it 'had completely different views on what it entailed'. Pre-echoes there as well, perhaps. Third, he registers the importance of social and economic factors in stimulating Catholic disaffection, and the increasing Protestant alienation from political developments (and even from politics itself) since the 1985 Anglo-Irish Agreement: neither of these stimulants to anger is easily written out of Northern Ireland's immediate future.

The book is a good one. I did, however, have some reservations. In places the narrative would surely have benefited from a greater emphasis on analysis. There is, for example, a very good record of Terence O'Neill's project, but little in the way of assessment. The same is true of the passage on the Anglo-Irish Agreement, of the section on community relations in recent years, and so on over numerous other important topics. More specifically, I feel that while people's activities and opinions are reported extremely well, there is little explanation of precisely *why* people did what they did, or felt what they felt with such strength of emotion. The material on, for example, Civil Rights activists such as Bernadette Devlin or Michael Farrell could have been more powerful if the unique complexity of their developing views had been unveiled, and if the specific influences which moulded their ideas had been explained. Moreover, the book as a whole lacks a defining argument. Dr Hennessey suggests in his Preface that, if there is a central theme in the work, 'it is that many of the events chronicled, whatever the intended goal of a particular policy, were interpreted by unionists and nationalists according to their particular world views'. This is no doubt true, but it is also profoundly obvious. Perhaps the author was keen to remain neutral, and therefore submerged his own analysis for the purposes of even-handedness. This is sometimes seen as an advantage in general histories, and perhaps it is. The book is certainly fair-minded and a very useful contribution to the literature. But would a sharper analytical knife not have made it more incisive?

Hennessey notes Ulster unionists' fundamental and lasting opposition to the Anglo-Irish Agrement. Unionist campaigns against the 1985 accord, and what it stood for, are the subject of Feargal Cochrane's welcome book on Unionist politics. Cochrane analyses the evolution of unionist politics from that dread November day until the present, and does so with considerable skill. The book's central argument is that 'the diversity of the [unionist] ideology's social composition is both its strength and its weakness'. Unionism's broad church quality has enabled it to possess impressive power, but has also led to its having proved immobile and negative. Cohesion can be maintained in opposition to unwanted developments; but disintegration occurs as soon as more positive directions are to be proposed and followed.

The book is based in part on interesting interviews with a range of politicians, whose views are undoubtedly varied: 'Unionist ideology contains diverse interest groups with little in common other than a commitment to the link with Britain.'

As Cochrane ably shows, unionists offer a variety of differing views concerning what the union is actually for. But is there anything surprising about this? Do not many (perhaps most) political movements contain members with a wide variety of opinions? Indeed, as Dr Cochrane demonstrates, the striking thing about unionist opposition to the Anglo-Irish Agreement was in fact how overwhelmingly widespread it was among the unionist community.

As with Hennessey's book, I found my admiration complemented by some doubts. Cochrane argues that, 'Clearly it can be seen that the unionist ideology is diverse to the point that it defies categorization.' But is this true? It might defy categorization according to strict social scientific typologies, but the problem there could well lie with the attempt to squeeze messy human experience into overly neat categories. Again, the author suggests that the central genius of the Anglo-Irish Agreement was that it did not rely on local support for its maintenance and that, as a consequence, it could withstand the predictable opposition of the unionist community. But is this not precisely the problem with the accord: for how can an agreement which predictably outraged the majority of a region's population be expected to hasten peace in that region?

Cochrane's book helpfully brings out the diversity and sincerity of unionist beliefs in Northern Ireland. Extremely helpful, too, is Henry Patterson's new edition of *The Politics of Illusion*. Initially published in 1989, this excellent treatment of the Republican movement is here updated – with a chapter covering the 1990-96 period, and with a highly intelligent new Conclusion. Patterson's sophisticated analysis of Republican strategy demonstrates the ambiguous and contradictory nature of the 1990s Peace Process. And he provocatively points out that some who, in the 1990s, trace 'peace' back to supposedly key developments in the 1980s were woefully unaware of the significance of these developments in their commentary at the time. The book's Conclusion deals with some interesting Republican dissidents, and here it echoes the author's treatment, earlier in the work, of fascinating figures such as Peadar O'Donnell. Patterson suggests that leading contemporary Republicans have in fact been serious about building a new kind of strategy, but that this tendency has not been as strong as uncritical supporters of the Peace Process have claimed. The Gerry Adams approach has involved an attempt to build a new Sunningdale-type agreement, which would drive a wedge between unionists and the British and produce a transitional period on the way to Irish unity. The problem, as Professor Patterson observes, is that this strategy requires more from the British state than can be expected: 'the imposition of a "transitional" settlement against the wishes of Ulster unionists'.

Like Henry Patterson, John Darby is a respected and experienced commentator on Northern Irish politics. His *Scorpions in a Bottle* offers a brief and lucid introduction to Northern Ireland from an ethnic conflict perspective. It is pitched at those with little knowledge of the place, and contains an historical overview, some useful appendices, and pointers to other sources of information on the place. It also offers some broader lessons of the Northern Irish conflict. While Professor Darby is a judicious exponent of the ethnic conflict approach, I still found myself unpersuaded about this intellectual framework. What is it that this approach distinctively offers? Darby defines the term 'ethnic conflict' very broadly, so much so that it seemed to me that any perceived cause of the conflict could be shielded under its umbrella. So the distinctiveness does not lie there. Nor does it lie in the capacity to transfer insights learned in one ethnic conflict directly to another. As Darby shrewdly observes, this is not appropriate: 'It is never possible to apply a template from one country to another.' Nor is it easy to present Northern Ireland as divided neatly into different ethnicities anyway: 'One of the myths of the ideologues in Ireland is that of ethnic purity. . . . The myth of purity is indefensible. Northern Ireland, like most places, is a community of mongrels.'

RICHARD ENGLISH

Successive Reincarnations

Fintan Lane. *The Origins of Modern Irish Socialism 1881–1896.* Cork University Press. 1997. ISBN 1 85918 151 1. IR£45.00 hbk. ISBN 1 85918 151 X. IR£16.95 pbk.

This book investigates the fortunes of the socialist movement in Ireland in the decades before the foundation of the Irish Socialist Republican Party by James Connolly in 1896. The introductory section traces the development and decline of Utopian socialism in the 1820s and 1830s and the turbulent reception given to the First International in the early 1870s. The main portion of the book details the successive attempts made – mostly in Dublin – to set up socialist organisations, beginning with the Democratic Federation of 1881 (later the Social Democratic Federation), moving through the Dublin Democratic Association, the Saturday Club and the Socialist League of 1885, the National Labour League, the Dublin Workingmen's Club and the Dublin Socialist Club (all in 1887), the Irish Socialist Union (1890), the Fabian Society (1892), culminating in the establishment of branches of the Independent Labour Party in Belfast (1892), Dublin and Waterford (both in 1894). This phoenix-like character of Irish socialism reflected both its tenacity and its inherent weakness. Identified with a pathetically small but determined circle of activists, and confined to a limited urban area, it *could not* survive undisturbed and *would not* simply die out, hence the successive reincarnations under different names which must surely have proved as confusing to contemporaries as they do to even the specialist reader.

One stated purpose of this book is to challenge the myth that Irish socialism began with Connolly. However, this is a myth which no longer exists – at least among labour historians – so perhaps the author was attempting to reinvent the wheel. However, this should not be allowed to detract from the value of the work, a value which consists in the painstaking exploration of hitherto shadowy areas of socialist development in Ireland, from the erratic growth of the Democratic Federation in the early 1880s to the building of the foundations for the Independent Labour Party a decade later. In fact this work is an excellent exercise in historical detection, unearthing the identities and activities of many 'unknowns' – artisans, labourers and clerks – whose socialist sympathies placed them outside the ranks of mainstream politics. It also fills a major gap in our understanding of the relationship between socialism in Ireland and elsewhere by charting the reaction to Irish affairs by a number of British and American socialist and radical thinkers and activists, from Hyndman of the Social Democratic Federation, through Henry George, the great exponent of land nationalisation, William Morris of the Socialist League, Will Thorne of the Gasworkers' Union and Keir Hardie of the Independent Labour Party.

A number of conclusions emerge from this study. Some, while presented as new findings, simply confirm what is already familiar to labour historians. For instance, it comes as no surprise that socialist ideas gained relatively little sympathy among trade unions and trades councils in Irish towns in the later nineteenth century. Neither is it unexpected that whatever socialist support did exist was confined largely to urban areas – particularly Dublin and Belfast though, as Lane also shows, sympathisers could be found in such unlikely outposts as Lurgan and Kilkenny. The reader is even less surprised to find that one of the main objections to socialism within Irish labour circles rested on the belief that socialism was synonymous with atheism, that Dublin activists deliberately avoided describing their organisation as 'socialist' so as not to frighten off potential recruits, or that Michael Davitt opposed the fusion of British and Irish trade unions so as to foster a home-grown labour movement.

Other points raised are far more thought-provoking: the strength of anarchist sympathies within Dublin's small socialist circle; the overlap between the Democratic Federation of the early 1880s and the Ladies' Land League; and the police authorities' fear in the mid-1880s that there was a link between socialism and separatism – something which hardly inspires confidence in the accuracy of the late nineteenth-century police report as a historical source. What makes particularly interesting reading is Lane's contention that while the vicissitudes of British socialism had a direct effect on the development of Irish socialist movements, influence also travelled in the opposite direction. More precisely, British socialism (or should we use the plural?) learned a great deal about the complexities of Irish politics from involvement with, for instance, the Irish land agitation in the early 1880s. Such close observation of the Irish situation by British socialist and radical activists also led to an increasingly favourable reaction to proposals for Irish Home Rule. This was motivated both by a reluctant admission of the perceived validity of Irish nationalist claims to self-government and by the wider view that Home Rule for Ireland would prove the thin end of the wedge which would destabilise and eventually shatter the empire.

Lane's attention to the emerging land agitation of the 1880s as the context in which Irish socialist ideas developed proves particularly enlightening. Although one could easily predict that Dublin socialism would prove to be strongly anti-farmer and that British socialists would look askance on the 'dismal road of peasant proprietorship' along which the Land League and its members travelled, one might not so easily deduce just how adamantly the Land League opposed land nationalisation and how contemptuous socialists and radicals from outside the island were regarding the mini-capitalist aspirations of land agitators. As Henry George, the American exponent of land nationalisation expressed it in 1881, it was 'as if a lot of small men had found themselves in the lead of a tremendous movement' and did not quite know how to cope with their new-found power – an astute observation of late nineteenth-century Irish socio-political realities, perhaps, but also an indication of the limitations of radical and socialist understanding of those same realities.

A word on sources. One aspect of this work which was quite irritating was its failure to fully mesh with the recently published work of other historians working in related fields. This is particularly evident in citations of some works published in the mid-1990s. The works appear in the bibliography but there seems to be no attempt to integrate their conclusions into the discussion in the main body of the text. This omission may go some way to explain why (as indicated earlier in this review) some relatively predictable conclusions are presented as novel and why there is such an imbalance in favour of Dublin. Where due cognisance was taken of other historians' work on, for instance, Belfast and Waterford, this imbalance was somewhat rectified – but not enough. Primary sources have, on the other hand, been handled not only painstakingly but also perceptively. The finecombing of the socialist and radical press – *Justice, Commonweal, Radical, Workers' Republic* (to name but a few) – has given insights almost totally denied to those who concentrate on the mainstream press, while the tapping of archival collections like the Henry George Papers, Marx Papers and William Morris Papers has allowed us to see Irish socialist developments from the vantage point of the interested outsider and against a much wider backdrop. Perhaps recourse might also have been had to some Catholic diocesan archives (Dublin, for instance) to let us see the question from the point of view of individual leading churchmen.

In his conclusion, Lane seeks reasons for the failure of socialism to gain any real headway in Ireland before 1896, and finds them in the interwoven issues of land, religion and nationalism. Few could take issue with this assessment in the light of Lane's research. The issue of land ownership in the 1880s beat the idea of land nationalisation into a very poor second place; the pursuit of Home Rule into the 1890s not only diverted nationalists (and labour activists) away from fundamental issues of social change but also alienated whatever Unionist support might have been forthcoming; and the suspicion of official church and pious laity regarding the 'godlessness' of socialism is not difficult to prove. But the reader is still left with a niggling suspicion that this three-pronged answer is still not wholly satisfactory. Does the failure of socialism have something to do with social and economic structures in Irish urban centres? Was the concept of 'class' incompletely formed in cities like Dublin, Cork and Belfast, still less in smaller centres? Or was it – as

Lane himself suggests – that Irish workers were just too firmly rooted in practicalities like housing, water schemes and employment conditions to get carried away by nebulous concepts like class?

MAURA CRONIN

Complex and Fascinating

Frank Callanan, *T. M. Healy.* Cork University Press, 1996. ISBN 1 85918 009 4. IR£25.00 hbk. ISBN 1 85918 172 4 IR£15.95 pbk.

Frank Callanan's *Healy* is three books in one. At the most obvious level it is a life of a controversial figure who was close to the centre of Irish nationalist politics for almost half a century. It is also a dual biography, a study of the interaction between Healy and the leader whom he loved and loathed; Parnell is a central character in his own right. And finally, a generous 150 pages are devoted to a detailed examination of Healy's rhetoric at the time of the split. In such a lengthy work there is space for a variety of themes and approaches, and in different ways all three aspects of the book make satisfying and even compelling reading. But they also make for an uneven finished product, and the whole is not greater than the sum of the parts.

Healy is an awkward subject for a biography. Like *Macbeth* he is a dramatic failure; he peaks too early, and in many respects the last forty years of his life are an anti-climax. The final section of the biography entitled 'After the Fall, 1891–1931', which amounts to little more than a third of the book, covers most of Healy's adult life. Here the author can do no more than make the most of the material provided for him by his subject's career.

But Callanan has imposed an extra burden on himself. He has already written a masterly study of the Parnell Split, and it is clear that he was anxious to avoid repeating himself in his later work. The result is that some material which had appeared already in his first book is excluded from the new biography. The results can be unfortunate, and on occasion he is disconcertingly brisk in his coverage of the events which formed the hinge of Healy's life.

For example, on p. 253 we learn that 'Healy, who had endorsed Parnell at a meeting in the Leinster Hall in Dublin on 20 November, crossed to London to rally the opposition to him'. Some pages later Healy is quoted as boasting about this speech, but we must turn to *The Parnell Split* to discover the full details: Healy dragged himself from his sick-bed to draft the resolution in Parnell's favour and to make the speech which was 'the definitive formulation of the case for Parnell. It was his last act as the master-propagandist of Parnellism, and contributed some of the stock phrases and images to Parnell's campaign in the split . . . It was an astonishing *tour de force* . . . It was a speech which Healy would never be permitted to forget'. Even when so many other details of Healy's career are provided in the biography, it is a pity to lose such a revealing incident.

But with only a few exceptions the portrait of a complex and fascinating man is painted with insight, with elegance, and with a convincing accumulation of detail. The range of sources used are a testament to the years during which Callanan tore himself from the Law Library to engage in archival research. Full justice is done to Healy's wit and flair, and his endearing characteristics are given proper weight. He emerges as a flawed but rounded character. Callanan provides convincing explanations for his successes and his ultimate, long-term failure, and he drives home the point that however unhappy Healy may have been as a team-player under Parnell, when left on his own without the leadership which he resented so deeply he became merely anarchic and destructive. The brilliant speaker became a barren politician who revelled in the role of pariah.

Callanan's treatment of the relationship between Healy and Parnell, the dual biography, is a formidable achievement. Although he does not disguise his admiration of Parnell's strategy and tactics, his distaste for Healy's vicious attacks is confined to the relevant sections of the book and he is careful to give his subject credit on the many occasions when it is due. The reader comes to share the author's relish for the intrigues, the enmities, the subterfuges and the betrayals of life in the Home Rule Party. Some of the minor characters come to life (Captain O'Shea and Henry Labouchere, for example), although others (John Redmond in particular) remain shadowy figures. Equally contagious is the author's increasing sense of exasperation with his two main characters, with their self-destructive faults, their blindness to each other's strengths and virtues, their inability to appreciate that their qualities complemented one another. Reading of the growing estrangement between them is like watching the break-up of a marriage. The reader can guess how Callanan would have voted in Committee Room 15, but he is scrupulously careful to appreciate the strengths in each side's case.

The most unusual aspect of the book is the detailed examination of the vituperative language which Healy used in denouncing Parnell and his followers. Healy's deconstruction of the Parnell myth is itself deconstructed under a range of different headings. This is done not only against the background of Healy's own character and preoccupations, but also in the light of an emerging Catholic, chauvinistic nationalism to which he was such a formidable contributor. Healy, and Irish affairs, are seen in a wider context

The book is long (perhaps too long) and, like most lives, it is uneven. Parts of it are brilliant. Callanan should be encouraged to continue his dual life, and (like Healy) to combine his legal practice wth the writing of history.

MICHAEL LAFFAN

Notes on Contributors

CHRIS AGEE works in Belfast for the Open University. His Bosnian anthology is published by Bloodaxe.

PEGGY BUTCHER is drama editor with Faber and Faber.

NEIL BUTTIMER lectures in Irish at University College, Cork and is editor of *Cork: History and Society* (1993).

MARINA CARR is a playwright. Her work includes *The Mai* (1994).

CIARAN CARSON's latest collection is *The Star Factory* (1997).

MAURA CRONIN lectures in history at Mary Immaculate College, Limerick and is the author of *Country, Class or Craft? The Politicisation of the Skilled Artisan in Nineteenth-Century Cork* (1994).

ALEX DAVIS lectures in the Department of English, University College, Cork and is co-editor of *Modernism in Ireland* (1995).

GEORGE T. DEMPSEY is a retired US diplomat.

RICHARD ENGLISH is Reader in Politics at Queen's University, Belfast and author of *Ernie O'Malley: IRA Intellectual.*

CARMEL FARRELLY is completing a Ph.D. on Anna and Thomas Haslam at University College, Cork.

ROY FOSTER is Carroll Professor of Irish History at the University of Oxford. His books include *W.B. Yeats: A Life – I: The Apprentice Mage, 1865–1914* (1997).

VONA GROARKE's last collection was *Shale* (Gallery Press, 1994). Forthcoming from the same press is *Poems about Houses* (provisional title).

KLAUS GUNNAR SCHNEIDER is a research student at the University of Kiel.

RICHARD KIRKLAND teaches English at Keele University.

MICHAEL LAFFAN lectures in Modern Irish History in University College, Dublin and is author of *The Resurrection of Ireland: the Sinn Féin Party 1916–23* (forthcoming, Cambridge).

JOEP LEERSSEN is Professor of European Studies at the University of Amsterdam. His books include *Remembrance and Imagination: Patterns in the Historical and Literary Representation of Ireland in the Nineteenth Century* (1996).

WILLY MALEY lectures in English at the University of Glasgow. He is the author of *Salvaging Spenser: Colonialism, Culture and Identity* (1997).

PATRICK MAUME is a research fellow in the Department of Politics at Queen's University and biographer of Daniel Corkery and D.P. Moran.

LEON MCAULEY is a poet, broadcaster and photographer.

FRANK MCGUINNESS lectures in English at University College, Dublin. His most recent play was *Mutabilitie.*

VIC MERRIMAN teaches drama at University College, Cork and chaired the Arts Council Theatre Review 1995-96.

JUSTIN QUINN published a collection of poems The *'0' o' a' a' Bird* (1997), is editor of *Metre* and teaches in Charles University, Prague.

DAVID WHEATLEY's first collection, *Thirst*, won the 1998 Rooney Prize for Irish literature. He is an editor of *Metre.*